HELLO THERE!

And welcome to our 14th Blue Peter Book. We're not boasting, but we do think we must have set a record. We can't think of any other programme on television that's had a book written all about it every year since 1963. On top of that, the books have been best sellers. Nearly half a million copies have been printed of each edition of books four to fourteen. And in the world of publishing, for hard-back books, this really *is* a record.

People often write and ask how they can get hold of books One, Two, Three, Four and Five.

The answer is—we just don't know. All the early editions are out of print and the only hope is to get one as a swap, or find one at a jumble sale. We keep one complete set in the Blue Peter office, and we'd very much like to hear from anyone else who's also got volumes One to Fourteen. If you *have*, our advice is hang on to them—they look as though they're well on their way to becoming real collectors' items! In the end they may be very useful, too. John Craven's set of *Eagle* annuals helped to raise funds for our Lifeline Lebanon Appeal.

DO YOU RECOGNISE ANY OF THESE PHOTOGRAPHS?

There's news of our Appeal on page 30, and now your collection of old stamps and postcards has brought badly needed help to thousands of babies and children who were victims of the terrible civil war in the Lebanon. Once more, a big "thank you" for every single donation—large or small.

We're very pleased to welcome a Neanderthal boy to our 14th book. Littlenose is a great favourite on *Jackanory*, and you can read his brand-new Ice Age adventure on page 34.

Our travels have taken us literally all over the world since book Number 13. And we've not only travelled far and wide, we've travelled *fast*. When Lesley was invited to be one of the VIP guests on board Concorde's inaugural flight from London to Washington, she flew 3,658 miles in 3 hours 49 minutes!

One of our new ideas this year has been our Blue Peter Special Assignment Twin Town series. If *your* town is twinned with one in a foreign country, you might have seen it on our films. We visited Warsaw, Coventry, Heidelberg, Cambridge, Fontainebleau, Richmond, Bordeaux, Bristol, Haifa and Portsmouth—and enjoyed every trip. What with that, and the new Go with Noakes series, *and* 80 twice-weekly editions of Blue Peter, we've hardly had time to draw breath. But the thing that makes it all worth while is getting your letters after the programmes. So keep on writing to us and telling us all the things you'd like to see—and don't forget the competition on page 77!

Peter Purves   John Noakes   Lesley Judd

Petra   Shep   Jack and Jill

THEY'VE ALL BEEN IN BLUE PETER. TURN TO PAGE 76 FOR THE ANSWERS.

PORRIDGE

"Red light and bell!"
"Quiet, please——"
"Turn over——"
"Speed."
"Mark it."
"*Porridge*. Scene 41. Take 1."
"Action!"
"Harris, stand still."
"What me, Mr MacKay?"
"Yes, you——"

The clang-clang of boots rang out along the iron balcony as Senior Prison Officer MacKay bore down on the trembling figure of Harris.

"Cut!" said the director, Syd Lotterby, and turned to the cameraman.

John McGlashan cut the camera motor and took his eye from the eyepiece.

"Do I have enough overlap with the previous shot?" asked Syd.

"I reckon you should be OK," McGlashan said.

Syd turned to the sound recordist.

"OK for you?"

Ron Blight took off his headphones and put his thumb up.

"Right—print that! Thank you, gentlemen. Get set up for Scene 42."

Suddenly pandemonium broke out as 50 people, unknown to the viewers but vital to the film, sprang into action. Lights had to be changed, scenery moved, actors' make-up repaired and cameras reloaded. During the "take" the whole studio had been silent apart from the voices of the actors. Now everyone was talking at once.

The place was Stage 3B on the set of *Porridge* at the BBC Television film studios in Ealing. As they set up Scene 42 of *Porridge*, I wondered just how many times the clapper-board had been heard at the Ealing film studios.

The BBC bought the place in 1956 and since then they must have filmed thousands of productions and millions of scenes. But before the BBC moved in, big films for the cinema were being made in these studios.

When I first came here I thought it looked more like a small family printing works than a great motion-picture studio. The whole place has a very modest English air, and the cinema films it turned out were very English, too. You still see them occasionally on television—films like *The Cruel Sea, Kind Hearts and Coronets, The Lavender Hill Mob* and *The Man in the White Suit.*

Thirty years ago Ealing studios started a unique brand of British comedy, and though it's made for a smaller screen, I think that *Porridge* has got a lot in common with those great Ealing films.

The next morning, at 9 o'clock, I found Ronnie Barker, Syd Lotterby, and John McGlashan watching their "rushes" in a tiny cinema next door to the studio. "Rushes" are prints of the film they'd shot the day before which had been "rushed" back from the laboratories to the studios. All the scenes were in a higgledy-piggledy order, and without sound, so it was only people who were working on the film who could make head or tail of them.

2215, Fletcher N. S., alias Ronnie Barker—
Britain's most popular prisoner.

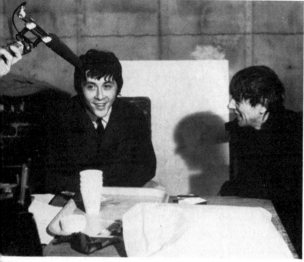

3751, Godber L. A., alias Richard Beckinsale—
Britain's most popular prisoner's mate.

Senior Prison Officer MacKay, alias Fulton Mackay,
the screw you love to hate.

For Ronnie, Syd and John it was their last chance to decide if yesterday's filming was good enough, or if they had to shoot it again today. Tomorrow would be too late, because the whole of Slade Prison was due to be demolished to make room for the next production.

"I think I should have moved a bit quicker there," said Ronnie, looking critically at himself on the silent screen.

"Don't worry, I can cut away earlier," said Syd, putting down his coffee. "Come on, they're all waiting for us in the studio."

Whilst Syd was setting up his first sequence, I managed to grab Ronnie for a quick word. We were high up in the gantry—a narrow platform—looking down at the studio.

"Syd's very good, you know," he said. "He's got it all under control."

Down on the studio floor, Syd whipped off his large horn-rimmed glasses.

"Fulton, can I see your walk once again—it might be a bit too long. Quiet, everybody. The red light is on."

"Just one thing, Syd, before you shoot," Ronald Lacey, the actor playing Harris, was saying. "When exactly do you want me to turn my head?"

While Syd was sorting out his problems, I asked Ronnie if he was ever embarrassed by being recognised in the street.

He said: "Well, a chap came up to me once and said:—'I know you.' 'Oh yes', I replied. You never know quite what to say, do you? The chap looked at me again and said: 'It's television, isn't it?' I said: 'That's right'. He said: 'It's still not working, you know!' He thought I was a technician who had delivered a television set to his house!"

We smothered another laugh, and I went off to have a look round the studio before I got into trouble.

Walking on the studio set was a remarkable experience. One moment I was in a tatty tangle of light cables running behind hardboard walls propped up by braces and weights, then I walked two paces and I was inside the familiar walls of Slade Prison. Those cold, shiny, forbidding walls looked uncomfortably real until I tapped them and discovered they were made of fibreglass. The prison gantries were real enough—all made of solid metal to give that ring of boots on iron that typifies a prison scene. And the back wall that is always seen in the distance looked every bit as solid, until I saw someone walk past carrying a camera tripod—and the whole wall wafted in the breeze. It was a hand-painted cloth!

Fulton Mackay, who plays Senior Prison Officer MacKay, is the man you love to hate: a diminutive figure, puffed up by his own importance and really enjoying putting "the screw" on Fletcher and the other prisoners.

I asked him if real prison warders recognised themselves in his performance. He laughed and gave that cocky tilt of the head that typifies MacKay.

"I think that *prisoners* recognise me more than the warders."

I found Syd lying down on Fletcher's bunk having a quiet look at the script before the next take, and I asked him if he'd ever been inside a *real* gaol. He told me about a visit he'd made recently to Lewes Prison.

"The governor said he now answers the stock question—'What's it like in gaol?' with 'Well, don't you ever watch *Porridge*?'"

Slade Prison may be made of fibreglass and timber but every Friday, at half-past eight, it's a real place for the 15 million people who laugh, and may even shed an occasional tear, whilst Fletcher is doing his Porridge.

Syd Lotterby, the director, who used to be a camera-man, received an Academy award for *Porridge*.

John McGlashan, the cameraman, gets ready for a "take".

Slade Prison is made out of fibre glass and timber, but once a week it becomes a real place for 15 million viewers.

THE YEAR OF THE SNAKE

The year of the snake was the year of the dragon for us. We'll never forget the day our studio was "invaded" by this magnificent 140-foot dragon powered by 80 pairs of feet.

The feet were human ones. They belonged to members of London's Chinese Community who later performed a spectacular Dragon Dance under the gaze of the lions in Trafalgar Square.

Dancing Dragons are always made especially for one dance, to celebrate a happy occasion and bring good luck by scaring away evil spirits. And our dragon celebrated a *double* event—the Chinese New Year and the Queen's Silver Jubilee, and it was the first full-sized dancing dragon ever to be shown in Europe.

The dancers themselves are underneath the wavy bamboo frame of the body. Holding it up is very hard work. For instance, the tail has to do a fantastic amount of running, because it has to twist and turn more than any other part of the body. It's held up by just one man—who takes turns with five others—swapping over as the dance goes on.

But most impressive of all was the gigantic head with its curling horns and snarling teeth. The pupils of the eyes had to be left unpainted when the dragon

came to the studio. The Chinese say it's very bad luck for a ceremonial dragon to see before the actual day of the dance it's been made for. And because that meant the dragon was sightless and could bite and kill, the eyes had to be covered up. Once the pupils are painted in, the dragon becomes good and friendly.

The head, which is strapped to the body, is worked by the leader of the dance. He communicates with the tail end by a series of complicated signals. He has to be quite an acrobat, too, because as he dances along he plays with

a large pearl symbol carried on a pole by another dancer.

By tradition, the pearl—the most precious stone—starts inside the dragon. The dragon spits it out, and as he begins to play with it, so the dance begins. The climax of the dance is when the dragon finally swallows the pearl.

Another tradition is that before the day the dragon's been made for, the head and the body must never dance together. But we were lucky. The Chinese very kindly agreed that they could dance separately.

If you missed the programme, these pictures will show you it was a truly incredible sight!

SIX BRAVE MEN

When I went by hovercraft across the Channel on a day trip to Calais, I had my photo taken in front of a huge statue in the main square. It was made by the famous sculptor Auguste Rodin, and it commemorates an event that's famous in the history of both England and France.

It's a grim sort of statue—six sad men in rags with ropes round their necks. Once, in real life, they stood in just this way on this very spot; only on *that* day the square was crowded with starving Frenchmen and outside the city walls King Edward III of England was waiting with his army. The men were the famous Burghers of Calais. This is their story.

Edward III of England was a great king and a mighty warrior. His mother was a French princess of the royal Blood, so he claimed to be the rightful King of France as well.

2 In 1346 he crossed the Channel with his army to back up his claim. At a place called Crécy, a terrible battle took place. The French fought bravely, but the English were stronger. The way lay clear for King Edward to take the town of Calais.

When the citizens saw the English army coming, they closed the gates and manned the walls. "We'll let no Englishmen enter *our* town," they cried.

4 King Edward was angry. He ordered a siege. His army surrounded the town. No food, no troops, no messages were to be allowed in or out of the gates. The siege went on for nearly a year.

Queen Philippa crossed from England to join her husband. She stayed in the camp with him—but all the time the King grew more angry with the citizens of Calais for holding up his conquest of France.

6 Inside Calais the people were desperate. Their clothes were in rags and they were starving. They thought themselves lucky if they caught a rat to eat. The governor wrote to the King of France, begging him to send help.

7 The message was carried secretly through the English lines, but though the people of Calais waited and hoped—no help ever came.

8 One day, an English flag was seen flying over Calais. It was a token of surrender. The gates opened and a messenger came to tell the King resistance was at an end.

9 Coldly, the King demanded that the keys of the city be brought to him by six chief citizens. "They must come barefoot, in their shirts, and with ropes round their necks," he said.

10 When the people of Calais heard the news, they were horrified. Which of their Burghers could they send out to certain death?

11 One man, Eustache de Saint Pierre, the wealthiest man in Calais, spoke up bravely. "Six of us must go, to save the rest of the people. I will be the first."

12 Inspired by his example, another rich man stepped forward then two wealthy landowners. Then the Mayor, Jean d'Aire, spoke. "I have had a long and happy life in Calais. Now I am ready to die for the town."

3 Finally, a very young man joined them. "I will go," he volunteered. "I have no wife or children to mourn for me."

14 So roped together, the six Burghers of Calais appeared before King Edward. "Give me the keys," he cried, harshly, "then put them to death."

5 Queen Philippa pleaded with him. "Don't do anything so cruel or so unworthy," she begged. "For my sake—let these men go!"

16 For a moment the King was silent. Then he spoke. "You know I cannot refuse you anything you ask."

7 So the good Queen ordered warm coats to be brought for the six Burghers, and gave them food to take back to the starving townspeople. They thanked her and blessed her, and went safely back to their homes. The next day, King Edward rode into Calais and claimed it for his own. Two hundred years later, Calais became French again, and today there's just the statue in the square to remind you of the day when the Burghers made their brave sacrifice and Calais became an English town.

BRUNEI

"Having a marvellous time—wish you were here . . ."

That's what we put on our postcard to the Blue Peter office the day we arrived in Brunei. And it was true! After leaving a Britain sweltering in the worst drought for 500 years, it was sheer luxury to get caught in this tropical rainstorm. It took just four seconds for us to get soaked to the skin and we found later that 50 millimetres of rain had fallen in about 45 minutes.

The next day, though, we had to pinch ourselves to believe it had happened. The rain had disappeared and there wasn't a cloud in the sky. But that's Brunei all over—it's a land of contrasts. When we took a chopper ride to a remote jungle clearing, the Ibans in the long-house we visited had a brand-new colour TV! Just 40 minutes away from one of the world's most advanced natural gas refineries, the Punan tribe still make blowpipes. They're not for tourists, either—the Punans use them every day to hunt in the forest. And in the primitive village of Berbunut, where the people have been charcoal burners for hundreds of years, there's a radio telephone network so that the villagers can send an SOS for a doctor, or just chat to their friends.

Brunei's quite hard to spot on a map of the world. It's a Muslim country tucked away in Northern Borneo, 12,000 miles from Britain. It's about as big as Lincolnshire, and ninety per cent is thick, impenetrable jungle.

As we flew over it in our helicopter, the only gaps in the green leaves were cut by the broad sweep of the twisting rivers— and we comforted ourselves with the thought that if we crashed we could try and escape by building a raft. After we'd

My first blowpipe lesson—from the chief of the Puna tribe.

Hot, black and sticky after a day as charcoal burners mates.

Our Jungle Survival raft looked terrific . . .

. . . until we tried it out and nearly drowned Lesley!

Sago pudding as you've never seen it before.

...one on our Jungle Survival course with the Royal Brunei Malay Regiment, we weren't so sure! Our raft sank, Lesley nearly drowned, John had diarrhoea, and Peter got prickly heat. It was quite a relief to get back to the civilisation of Bandar Seri Begawan, Brunei's capital city, where preparations were in hand for a most spectacular ceremony. Brunei is a sultanate, and each year the celebrations for the Sultan's birthday last 40 days and 40 nights. On July 15th the Sultan, whose record-breaking name is *His Highness Sir Muda Hassanal Bolkiah Mu'izzaddin Waddaulah*, was 30 years old. There were parades and processions with stilt-walkers, jugglers and carnival floats, feasts, fireworks, a Royal Birthday March Past—rather like our Trooping the Colour—ending with a fly-past by the Imperial choppers, saluting their Sultan with trails of coloured smoke; and a competition for the best floodlit building—won when we were there by Brunei's TV Centre!

One of the biggest surprises we had on our expedition was discovering that sago starts off as sawdust. It comes from the Sago Palm tree and, after the wood is cut, the sawdust is soaked in water. As the water is squeezed out, the sago particles go with it, but the squeezing isn't done by machinery, but by human feet—jumping up and down on top of the sawdust. The dried sago gets packed solid in palm-leaf containers and is exported all over the world. The Bruneians don't cook it in milk, like us. They eat little boiled cubes of it with their drinks—like oriental potato crisps—and it's a popular dish at wedding receptions where it's covered in a delicious caramel sauce.

We had some at the Malay wedding we were invited to—together with nearly two thousand other guests! And unlike a British wedding, every one eats *before* the ceremony and before the groom arrives. The groom's guests have their own separate party, and the actual wedding is the climax of several days of traditional ceremonies. The bride isn't supposed to smile—but we were all sure she'd enjoyed her day. It was certainly one of the best parties *we'd* ever been to.

Not a game for "It's a Knockout"—squeezing sago, Brunei fashion.

These Iban children may live in a long-house in the jungle—but they have colour TV.

15

GOOD MORNING! IT'S SWAP SHOP

When Noel Edmonds opened his Multi-Coloured Swap Shop I was very pleased to be invited to be one of his first guests.

It was great fun, and I swapped my smelly goat dung painting from the Ivory Coast in no time! But all the while I was chatting with Noel, I had half an ear open for the phone calls! People were ringing in non-stop, wanting to chat or swap, and I was fascinated to know how the phone-girls coped with all the calls. So much so that I asked if could come back again—not to appear on the telly, but to give a hand with manning the phones.

I turned up at 8.30 with ten other girls and had a quick lesson from Frances. I know her quite well, because the rest of the week she's the Blue Peter prop. buyer. That means she gets all the bits and pieces John, Peter and I need to do the programme from a simple pair of scissors to Coronation coach!

Although Swap Shop doesn't start till 9.30, the phones were already ringing—and they were being answered, too.

"What do I do?" I asked.

Frances showed me a special form I had to fill up when anybody rang.

"Whatever you do," she said, "fill it up properly—their name, their telephone number and wha they want to talk about. And whatever you do, DO IT RIGHT!"

So I put my earphones on, grabbed a pen and got to work.

"Good morning!" I said. "It's Swap Shop."

Little did I know I was going to say that 97 more times that morning! If you've ever tried phoning in and you've been one of the lucky ones that's got through to the studio, this is what happens when you ring. All the details of your call are noted down, and you're asked to ring off. Then, if you're chosen to speak on televison (and it's a bit like winning the pools if you're picked), the BBC rings you back so you don't have to pay for the call.

Over a thousand calls get through to the Saturday morning Swap Shop. Noel reckons to speak to about 30 people on Saturday mornings, and to get those calls on the air there's a lot of hectic work going on behind the scenes! And all morning, as the glamorous guests and the pop stars drifted in and out of the studios, we phone-girls were chatting on the phone non-stop. There was hardly a second to sip a cup of coffee, and certainly not a chance of getting an autograph!

"Well," said Noel, after the red light went out and the programme was off the air, "what was it like?"

"Great!" I said. "I really enjoyed it."

And I did, too—though for hours afterwards my ears were ringing and inside my head I kept saying to myself over and over again: "Good morning! It's Swap Shop!"

There are 10 phone lines to Swap Shop—all ringing non-stop! That equals a thousand calls every Saturday morning!

Frances showed me how to work the head-set and gave me my instructions.

Every caller is noted down on a special form—the name, what they want to talk about—and, most important, their telephone number.

Cathy and John sort the forms and pick out who's going to speak to Noel. If you're chosen from the hundreds of callers, you're as lucky as if you'd won the pools!

This is the "call back" section. If you're going to speak to Noel, the BBC rings you back so you don't have to pay for the call.

Malcolm, the Sound Supervisor, tests the lines to make sure the technical quality is good, and millions of viewers can hear what you've got to say.

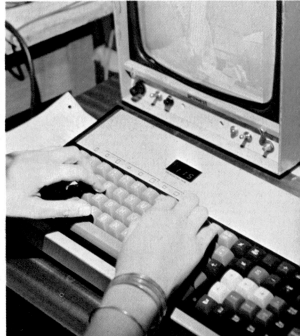

When the line's checked, Sheila types the name of the caller on her mini-computer.

Karen Edwards has got through! When Noel says "Who's that calling on line 2?" Karen's name will be put on your television screen.

Noel speaks to about 30 people in every programme, and funnily enough, it takes about 30 people behind the scenes in the studio to get each one on to the air!

"Did you enjoy it?" asked Noel when the show was over. "I can't hear you," I said. "After answering the phone 98 times, my ears are singing!" It was good fu though. Perhaps he'll ask me again!

Queen Elizabeth Slept Here

If you ever visit a stately home when you're on holiday, very likely the guide will tell you "Queen Elizabeth slept here".

If this has happened to you several times, you probably think to yourself "Queen Elizabeth seems to have got around!"

And she certainly did—probably more than any other Queen before or since.

Elizabeth I came to the throne when she was twenty-five. She reigned for forty-five years, and throughout her long reign she was tremendously popular with the ordinary men and women of the country.

She made up her mind that her people should have every chance of getting to know her, because then, she believed, they would stay loyal to her.

So every year, in the summer, she set out on her travels through the kingdom—these journeys were called the Queen's Progresses.

The Queen usually rode on horseback, with her courtiers attending her. To the crowds who lined her way, she seemed like a being from another world.

"God Save Your Grace!" they shouted.

"God save my people!" she replied.

Every town expecting to receive her swept the streets and decorated the houses, and the chief citizens were lined up to meet her.

They were expected to make the Queen a handsome present—once Coventry gave her a gold cup filled with one hundred pounds in gold.

When her travels took her to the University

The Queen and her court expected lavish banquets. Lord North and his wife had all this food prepared for a four day Royal visit.

The Earl of Hertford set three hundred men to work improving his grounds.

This was the transformation scene when the Queen arrived.

towns of Oxford and Cambridge, the students put on plays in Latin for the Queen's amusement. Some of the courtiers found this extremely heavy going, but the Queen, who was very learned, delightedly made speeches of thanks—in Latin, too!

The Queen didn't wait to receive invitations—she invited herself. It was considered a great honour, so any nobleman who was informed that the Queen intended to stay at his house was very flattered, but very nervous, too. Everything had to be *just* right to please Her Majesty, and it would certainly all be terribly expensive.

Weeks ahead, the Queen's hosts began to make plans for a royal welcome. When Lord North of Kertlinge was expecting the Queen for a four-day visit, he had prepared:

    74 barrels of beer
     6 barrels of claret
    20 gallons of sack
    32 swans
    34 pigs
    32 geese
     4 stags and 16 buck
  176 pasties—
together with gulls, snipe, plover, curlews, oysters, crayfish and herring.

And in four days Elizabeth and her court ate the lot!

When Lord Egerton entertained the Queen, after a great banquet he and his family appeared, all bearing gifts for her. There was a handsome fan set with diamonds, a nosegay holding a rich jewel, a fine silk and velvet gown, and a musical instrument called the virginals.

Preparations for the Queen's amusement were just as elaborate.

The Earl of Hertford set three hundred men to work, improving his grounds and digging out a lake with three islands. When the Queen arrived, sea gods and monsters were swimming in the lake, circling round a company of men who pulled an ornamental boat, with an orchestra and choir aboard.

The Queen was delighted!

Of course, the entertainments didn't always happen as planned.

Once, a tableau of twelve nymphs was arranged by a pool, ready to sing and dance to greet the Queen. There was a clap of thunder—a heavy shower—the nymphs got soaking wet, and the Royal Visitor hurried past without even a glance.

Though she enjoyed all this lavish hospitality, it was contact with the common people the Queen valued most.

One day, when she was travelling in her coach, a man in the crowd shouted to the Royal Coachman, "Stop thy cart, good fellow, so that I may speak to the Queen!" The Queen roared with laughter, for however haughty she was with the nobility, she was always very gracious to her poorer subjects.

The courtiers, unlike the Queen, did *not* enjoy the Progresses. At night, when they were tired out, many of them had to lodge in uncomfortable little attics, because all the best rooms were full. Then, when the party was due to move on, there was a terrible bustle and confusion. All the Queen's luggage, with her elaborate dresses and finery,

had to be loaded on to slow, lumbering carts to get to the next stopping place before she did.

But she often changed her mind, and sometimes, when all the luggage had gone ahead, a message would arrive from Her Majesty to say she had decided to stay on!

The arrangements were bound to be complicated. In one typical year, the Queen left London on 11 July to travel through Essex, Suffolk and Hertfordshire.

She visited Lord Rich, Sir John Grey, Sir William Petre, and Lord John Darcy. She stopped at Chelmsford, Colchester, Harwich and Ipswich—and many other places besides.

Amazingly, everything worked to plan, and she got back to London safely on 12 September—nine weeks later. The courtiers were worn out, but Queen Elizabeth was still as fresh as a daisy.

The Queen's Progresses were her summer holidays, when she travelled into the countryside and got to know her subjects, and she loved every minute of them!

Orange Delight

You don't eat it—you smell it!
It's an Elizabethan Pomander and it's very
easy to make. All you need is a small, firm
orange, the cheapest cloves you can get from a
chemist, a bit of talcum powder, a paper bag
and some patience! Follow these instructions
and you'll end up with a present for a lady that not
only looks good, but smells delicious! Why not try it?

1 Use a nail or knitting needle to make holes through the orange skin. Don't put them too close.

2 Divide the orange in quarters with cotton tape. Hold in place with a pin.

3 Start by pushing the cloves in along the line of the tape. Then, for a nice finish, try to fill the space with neat rows.

4 Fill in the holes with cloves. The orange will shrink when it dries, so the cloves will end up close together.

Put the clove-covered orange in a paper bag (plastic won't do) and shake some talcum powder in with it. The cheapest unscented kind is best. Put the bag in a warm, dry place, like the airing cupboard. LEAVE FOR SIX WEEKS. When you open the bag, you'll find the orange is smaller, lighter, and quite dry. Shake off the talcum powder. Unpin the cotton tape and get decorating! I've used left-over bits of ribbon and braid. Glue or pin them into place. (By the way, if you use pins, keep the pomander away from the baby.) When you've finished, you'll have an attractive scented pomander which will make an ideal present. And if you put a loop on top, you can hang it on the Christmas tree, all ready to give on Christmas Day.

John and Pete both went to see me off at London Airport—and then dashed back to the studio.

But before they'd got to Television Centre at Shepherds Bush, I would be half way to America!

 On Friday, 14 May, I walked in to the Blue Peter office to collect my script for the following Monday, and to have a chat with the producers and directors.

As soon as I opened the door, I knew that something was up.

The office is usually a fairly busy place on Friday afternoons, but that day it was in an uproar. Every phone was in use and the place was bursting with people all waving their arms about and talking at once. Biddy Baxter was in the middle of a phone call to America when she saw me standing in the doorway.

"Oh, Lesley," she said, "I'm so glad you've come. On Monday week you're flying to America in Concorde."

"But you're coming back to film in Hyde Park the next day," said John Adcock, the film producer.

From that moment I was part of a huge team mounting the biggest operation in the history of Blue Peter. There were meetings with British Airways to settle all the flight details. A top Outside Broadcast producer was despatched to Washington to take charge of the American cameras which were to cover the landing at Dulles Airport, whilst a crack London unit was sent to Heathrow to shoot the take-off. A communications satellite orbiting the earth had to be "booked" to beam the pictures back from America to the Blue Peter studio.

The idea was for John and Pete to do the really

difficult job of making a live commentary from the Blue Peter studio whilst lucky Lesley Judd flew in extravagant luxury in Concorde, along with a whole plane-load of VIPs.

If all went according to plan, I was to get off the plane in Washington where I would be handed a microphone, walk to a prearranged spot—and talk to you in Britain!

My alarm clock went off at 6 o'clock on the morning of Monday, 24 May, and I thought, "Gosh, I'm doing Blue Peter from America today!" I still couldn't believe that *I*, Lesley Judd, was going to take part in a piece of history. In a few hours' time I would be breaking the sound barrier, establishing a world record, and travelling as fast as a bullet leaves a rifle.

John and Peter came to the airport to see me off. When we said goodbye, I had the feeling I was going away for ever, like the Pilgrim Fathers, and yet I would be seeing them both the following day!

 The last John and I saw of Lesley was a little figure giving us a wave through the crack between the loading ramp and the door of Concorde.

From the airport roof we watched the great white bird taxi to the end of the runway, hesitate for a second, and then, with a roar you feel with every nerve in your body, she streaked down the tarmac and soared into the air. She may not be the quietest aeroplane in the world, but she's certainly the most beautiful.

The time was one minute past one and Lesley

Back in the Blue Peter studio, we watched the historic satellite pictures of Concorde's arrival in Washington.

I was about to make Blue Peter's first "live" direct broadcast from the United States of America.

was due to land in Washington, three and a half thousand miles away, in less than four hours' time. But before that happened, we had to get back to the studio to do the rest of Blue Peter.

 Whilst John and Peter were grabbing a coffee and a bun at the TV Centre, I was zooming away, sipping a glass of champagne and tucking into a juicy steak off a bone-china plate as we sped across the Atlantic at 1350 mph.

 We started the programme by showing a recording of the take-off, and then a few minutes later we were getting the first pictures of Concorde as it made its approach to Dulles Airport in Washington. It began as a small dot appearing out of the heat haze, which slowly grew and changed into the unmistakable shape of Concorde.

Seven minutes after the British Concorde took off from London, her opposite number, the French Concorde, left Paris. They were 12 minutes apart all the way across the Atlantic, with the two captains in touch with each other by radio.

Pete and I both felt a lump rising in our throats when we saw our plane, with Lesley in it, touch down at Washington. Minutes later the French Concorde appeared over the horizon and at 5.00 p.m., exactly as planned, both these magnificent aircraft were standing nose to nose in front of the airport terminal.

Then we waited for what seemed like hours for Lesley to appear on the tarmac. We chatted away as we watched the great mobile transit lounge creep up to the aircraft door to take the other passengers off. Pete pointed out that the steps which had been specially arranged for Lesley were locked into position. But no Lesley. . . !

Then, when we'd said everything we knew about Concorde, the Captain, the crew, and even the passengers—several times—we heard a small, worried, familiar voice coming from the direction of the aircraft. But there was still no sign of the body!

 What they didn't know was—I was stuck! I had just flown the Atlantic in 3 hours, 49 minutes and 32 seconds in the most sophisticated aircraft ever

invented. Everything was planned down to the last detail, but the kitchen door was stuck! It had been carefully arranged that I was to make a quick get-away through the kitchen and down a special flight of steps, but I just couldn't get through the door.

I knew that John and Pete would be going frantic back in the Blue Peter studio so I took a pace back and hurled all 51 kilos of me at the door, and, to my everlasting relief, it opened.

 It wasn't only to *her* everlasting relief, either! I don't think Pete and I have ever been so pleased to see Lesley since she first came on the programme.

And after the relief I'm not ashamed to say I felt a really great thrill of pride for Concorde, for British aviation, for the BBC Outside Broadcast department—and for Blue Peter—when I heard Lesley say:

"This is Lesley Judd speaking to you live from Washington's Dulles Airport for Blue Peter's first-ever direct transmission by satellite from the United States of America."

To prove I'd been there, I had my picture taken in front of the Capitol building in Washington.

Concorde

... the world's most advanced airliner which travels faster than a rifle bullet at twice the height of Mount Everest.

Key To Numbers.

(1) The fuselage, the main body of Concorde, consisting of a long slender aluminium alloy cylinder, tapered at each end to reduce drag. Air inside it is pressurised as Concorde flies high above the normal atmosphere. (2) The nose cone, a hinged drop-down section known as the 'droop snoot'. (3) Weather-detecting radar equipment. (4) Visor, made of reinforced glass, which is raised to cover the windscreen to give a more streamlined shape at high speeds. (5) The flight deck from which the aircraft is controlled. Crew normally consists of a pilot, co-pilot and an engineer. (6) Radio

and electronics compartment. (7) Forward galley space where meals are prepared. (8) Front passenger entrance. (9) Coat stowage compartment. (10) Toilet. (11) Forward cabin space. (12) Toilet compartments. (13) Middle passenger entrances on both sides. (14) Emergency radio stowage compartment. (15) Main cabin space. A maximum of 140 passengers altogether may be carried in the two cabins. (16) Rear entrance door. (17) Aft galley space, also containing first-aid equipment. (18) Baggage space.

(19) The wings. Concorde's beautiful wing shape has been specially designed

so that the aircraft flies steadily at all speeds ranging from 119 knots at take-off to twice the speed of sound. (20) Fuel tanks. Much of the wing is used to hold the 26,000 gallons (119,000 litres) of kerosene carried. (21) Forward wing tanks. Going supersonic alters the 'trim' or balance of the aircraft, and to help maintain the trim fuel is pumped from these tanks into (22), the aft trim tank. (23) Engine power is provided by four Rolls-Royce/SNECMA Olympus 593 turbo-jets slung under the wings, and which between them drink up 4¼ gallons of fuel per mile! (24) Reverser buckets—flaps

Geoffrey WHEELER

Who Makes What?

Concorde is built jointly between Britain and France. The nose and forward fuselage section, fuselage rear end with the tail and the engines are made in Britain. France takes care of the centre section of the fuselage, the wings and the undercarriage.

Facts and Figures

Wingspan 83 ft 10 ins (25·56 metres), length 202 ft 4 ins (61·66 metres). Weight, fully loaded at take-off, 400,000 lb (181,435 kg). Cruising speed Mach 2·05 (1,354 mph), a mile in less than 3 seconds, at 51,300 ft altitude. Maximum range 4,080 miles.

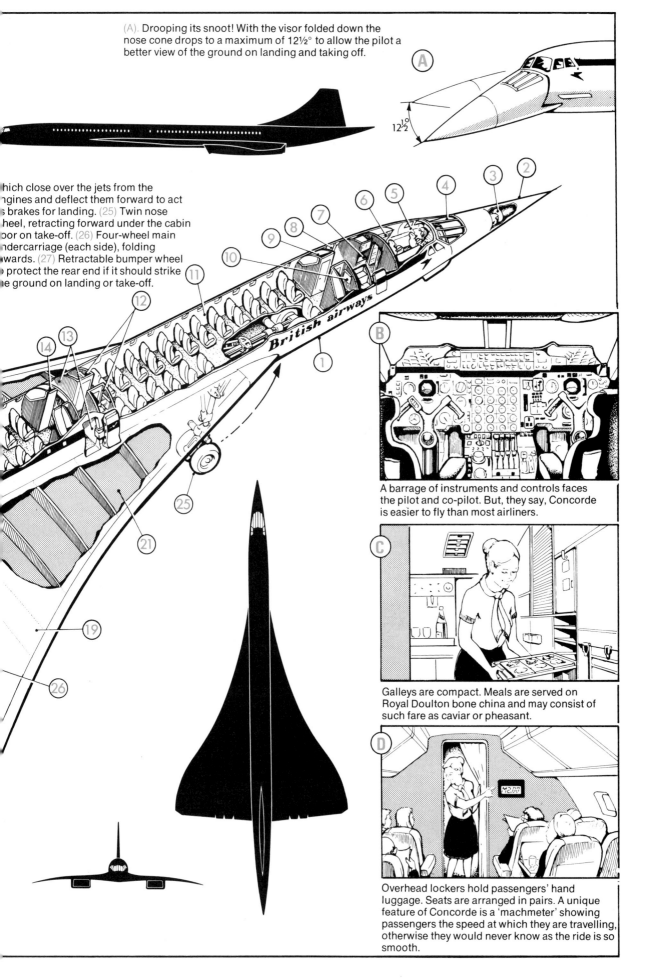

(A). Drooping its snoot! With the visor folded down the nose cone drops to a maximum of 12½° to allow the pilot a better view of the ground on landing and taking off.

12½°

...hich close over the jets from the ...gines and deflect them forward to act ...s brakes for landing. (25) Twin nose ...heel, retracting forward under the cabin ...oor on take-off. (26) Four-wheel main ...ndercarriage (each side), folding ...wards. (27) Retractable bumper wheel ... protect the rear end if it should strike ...e ground on landing or take-off.

British airways

A barrage of instruments and controls faces the pilot and co-pilot. But, they say, Concorde is easier to fly than most airliners.

Galleys are compact. Meals are served on Royal Doulton bone china and may consist of such fare as caviar or pheasant.

Overhead lockers hold passengers' hand luggage. Seats are arranged in pairs. A unique feature of Concorde is a 'machmeter' showing passengers the speed at which they are travelling, otherwise they would never know as the ride is so smooth.

27

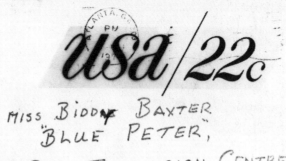

AIR MAIL

usa/22c

AEROGRAMME
VIA AIRMAIL
PAR AVION

Miss Biddy Baxter
"Blue Peter",
B.B.C. Television Centre,
London, W.12.
England.

When this airmail letter from Georgia, USA, arrived in the Blue Peter office, it gave us news of what we think is probably Petra's last surviving puppy, Candy.

The pups aged 5 days old, just before their eyes were open. Candy is at the bottom on the left.

Seven weeks old—left to right: Candy, Rover, Patch, Peter, Kim, Rex, Prince and Bruce.

If you have our Blue Peter Book number 3, you'll know that Thursday, 9 September 1965 is one of Blue Peter's most important anniversaries. It was the day that Petra's eight puppies were born at half-past three in the afternoon. Now, twelve years later, only Candy is left, 3000 miles away in the United States of America.

Candy was the first of the pups to leave the litter. Because she was friendly, we thought she'd fit in well in a home with plenty of people around, so we gave her to a Children's Home to be shared by all the people there who didn't have any other pets.

Candy was looked after by the children and the matron, Miss Phillips, and eventually, when Miss Phillips retired, so did Candy. And when Miss Phillips decided to go and live in Georgia, she couldn't bear to leave Candy behind, so they *both* emigrated!

As she was so friendly, we gave Candy to a Children's Home.

ording to the letter and the photos Miss s sent, Candy's in great form. And we wrote o Miss Phillips to say that, apart from her atism and her diabetes, Petra's not bad for old lady, either. After all—in human —she's a hundred and two and a half years andy's a mere eighty-four!

Miss Phillips' photographs of Candy in America with her friend Pedro.

Dear Miss Baxter,

As "Candy" is now in her twelfth year, I thought you might care to know how she is, apart from still having a beautiful coat (no grey hair) she is extremely fit with an abundance of energy like that of a two year old, it is hard to believe that she is nearly twelve; after a five mile walk she is still ready for more. When I take her for her shots to the vet, he calls her his ageless "friend".

"Pedro", my ten year old lab. is devoted to "Candy" and s. to him. he is also very fit, but app. as much older than Candy, which at times gets very frustrating for her when he is not always in the mood for a romp. I am also delighted that she has her figure still, I guess she has too much vitality to ever get fat. "Petra" must be about fifteen now. how is she?

my very best wishes to you and all the Blue Peter team.

Yours sincerely.

Joyceen Phillips.

Candy and Pedro.

LIFELINE LEBANON

Last November this brave group of people paid a flying visit to the Blue Peter studio on their way to London Airport. There were four nurses and a doctor—members of the first-ever British medical team allowed into the battle area of war-stricken Lebanon. They were taking a vital lifeline to more than a hundred thousand injured and homeless babies and children who were victims of the terrible civil war, but there was one big snag—due to shortage of funds, their resources and medical supplies would only last for three months. After that, the team would have to return to Britain, leaving thousands of sick children without care. Somehow, we had to extend that lifeline—but how?

Pictures like this left us in no doubt that our Lifeline was desperately needed.

"Our Stampede stamps were very successful," Peter said.

"And so was our Clothes-horse Race wool and cotton, and the buttons, badges and buckles for our 3 Bs Appeal," said Lesley.

John pulled his fingers through his hair, which he always does when he's thinking. "Stamps are good because they don't weigh much—but we ought to try and collect something different, too—something we've never asked for before. How about postcards?"

It was a brilliant idea. Old postcards are an up-and-coming collectors' item. They're light and easy to put in the post. We worked out you could put ten of them in an envelope and send it for the minimum postage rate of $6\frac{1}{2}$ pence. As many as 300

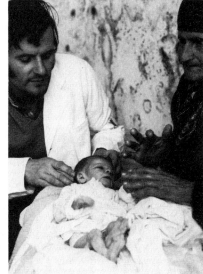

Some of the medical supplies provided by our Lifeline.

Nurse Mary Hawkins at work at
one of the Refugee camps.

Dr McInnes was the leader of the
Mercy Mission.

Our second Lifeline doctor.
Elizabeth Balmer from Yorkshire.

Sorting out the Lifeline Lebanon stamps and postcards was a colossal
task, but we managed to double our target and more.

used stamps could be sent for the same rate. If we asked Blue Peter viewers to collect postcards *and* stamps, we were sure we'd be well on the way to extending that badly needed lifeline.

We talked to Dr McInnes, leader of the Mercy Mission. He reckoned that the team needed to stay out in the Lebanon for a minimum of three extra months. On top of that they'd need extra medical supplies. He gave us a list—it was a *very* long one:

10 tons of dried skimmed milk
15,000 doses each of Tetanus vaccine
                       Cholera vaccine
                       B.C.G. (Tuberculosis)
                         vaccine
                       Polio vaccine
                       Measles vaccine
                       Penicillin tablets
Insulated bags to keep the vaccine at the right temperature
2 Sterilisers 2 Baby weighers
1 Haemoglobinometer for blood tests
50 Telescopic crutches
A stock of disinfectant, plaster of Paris, lint, cotton wool, bandages, safety-pins, and swabs

We did some rapid arithmetic and worked out how this could be achieved. The answer—by collecting *two million* envelopes full of old stamps and postcards.

Would we ever get them? We just didn't know—but at least we'd have a try.

The aim of our Lifeline Lebanon was to help babies and children on *both* sides—Moslems and Christians—all of them completely innocent victims of the war, so our team had to be divided into two.

Dr McInnes and Nurse Mary Hawkins (to be joined by Nurse Jane Barnes) would work at the Moslem refugee camps where more than 40,000 children were living eleven to twelve in a room in filthy conditions. Nurses Elizabeth Lamb, Margaret Poulton and Adrea Ripley would be on the Christian side in the Orthodox Hospital. Before they arrived there was only one nurse to look after all the children, yet an average of 80 new casualties were being admitted each night.

We said "goodbye" to the teams as they left for London Airport, and promised we'd try and keep in touch via the BBC's Middle East Correspondent, Chris Drake. This proved far more difficult than we'd imagined. Although a cease-fire had been declared, it was the fifty-fifth since the war had begun! The situation was still very tense and very dangerous, and it was incredibly difficult to make contact with Beirut, Lebanon's capital. But miraculously, during the four weeks before Christmas Chris Drake managed to send us his film reports.

They left us in no doubt as to how badly the Lifeline was needed.

We saw babies and children with bandages and dressings on their wounds that had not been changed for six months. Many of the children had terrible injuries caused by exploding bombs and gun fire, and collapsing buildings. Some were badly burned and others had been injured by walking on broken glass and rubble, for, unlike most wars, many of the battles of this civil war had been fought actually in the streets of Beirut, amongst the flats and houses, so children were an easy target. But apart from dressing the wounds and setting fractures there were dreadful problems of disease and malnutrition. Because most of the children had had insufficient food and drink they were quick to catch diseases. They were badly in need of vaccinations to prevent an outbreak of plague, and the babies were in desperate need of skimmed, dried milk. Chris not only managed to film the nurses and Dr McInnes in action, but on 3rd January 1977 he brought Dr McInnes to a telephone in Beirut so that we could speak to him "live" from the Blue Peter studio and give him the wonderful news that our target of 2,000,000 envelopes had been reached and that our Lifeline could be extended.

Dr McInnes was overjoyed. He said that now that most of the *injured* babies and children had been given the aid they needed, the team could concentrate on fighting the battles against disease and plague. This was a danger now the rainy season had begun because most of the streets were running with open sewers. Dr McInnes also told us he'd decided to hand over to another doctor who specialised in looking after babies and children—Dr Elizabeth Balmer from Yorkshire.

We learned after our programme that just one minute after we'd said "good-bye" the lines between Beirut and London were cut off. The government had imposed a state of emergency, and once more we'd lost contact with our teams. But luckily they were allowed to continue with their work, and although we'd reached our Target, your stamps and postcards still came flooding in. Nine weeks later, we'd reached a total of *five million* envelopes of donations. This meant that a colossal amount of additional aid could be given: two tons of special food, braces and leg irons for polio victims and spastics, the repair and re-equipping of the polio and spastics ward in the Ajazzi Hospital, the equipment for a training centre for the six- to fifteen-year-olds, and further supplies of badly needed vaccines, and a nursery for the under-fives.

Thanks to *you*, our Lifeline Lebanon has saved thousands of lives and rehabilitated thousands more.

PS. At our Lifeline Lebanon Auction on Tuesday 12th April 1977 the most valuable of your stamps and postcards were auctioned by Phillips of Bond Street. They raised the magnificent sum of £18,193.60p, all of which will help the children and babies who are so badly in need.

Delivery by chopper—the army lent a helping hand with stamps from children at Netheravon.

Ronnie Barker helped us reach our target with a magnificent album of old postcards.

NOW FOR TH GOURD NEWS

Do you have a monster in *your* garden? Mr Denis Moat of Canterbury does—this extraordinary plant with long creeper-like tendrils, some of them over 15 metres or 50 feet, and growing at the rate of 32 cms a day!

When we took Blue Peter cameras to film the monster we discovered it was rapidly taking over the entire garden. The gigantic tentacles had made mincemeat of Mr Moat's runner beans and roses, and were just about to seize his tomatoes and brussels sprouts. Every few metres there were mysterious fruits—looking like oversized gourds, and so heavy that Mr Moat had devised an ingenious method of supporting them. He put them in his wife's old tights hung from poles.

It all started in 1975 when Mr Moat planted some foreign seeds. Nothing happened and he forgot all about them, until May 1976 when he noticed some shoots coming through. With liberal doses of bath water and manure, they started growing rapidly, and after two months the first flowers and then the fruit appeared. Mr Moat's theory is that the combination of plenty of bath water and the long, hot summer had produced tropical forest-like conditions in his back garden. When he got in touch with experts at Kew Gardens, they were baffled. But they were certain of one thing—the monster fruit were definitely *not* poisonous.

With that assurance, Lesley bravely took a bite and found the fruit had a sweet and rather lemony flavour. But the mystery of the gourd remains—the Kew Gardens botanists think it's most likely to be a Cucurbita Ficifolia from East Asia, but they're still not absolutely certain.

Mr Moat has very kindly given us some seeds—but dare we plant them? They'd smother our Blue Peter garden in a matter of weeks—and then what? If the BBC's Television Centre was submerged under a mass of waving fronds and tentacles, we might be out of a job!

ROCK-A-BYE LITTLENOSE

Written and
illustrated by
John Grant

Night had fallen, and in the caves of the
Neanderthal Folk everyone was fast asleep.
Except Littlenose. He tossed and he turned. He sat
up in bed and lay down again. Until at length
Father shouted from the other end of the cave,
"For goodness sake, Littlenose, go to sleep and
stop fidgeting. You're keeping everyone awake."

This wasn't quite true, however, as Mother was
only awake because Father was shouting, and
Two-Eyes, Littlenose's pet mammoth, was fast
asleep in a corner, twitching his ears occasionally
as he dreamed mammoth dreams. But Father
wasn't bothered by details. He got out of bed and
went over to Littlenose's own special corner. In
the flickering light of the fire Littlenose looked up
at him from the middle of an untidy heap of fur
bedclothes.

"I can't get to sleep," he said plaintively. "My
bed's full of bumps and wrinkles."

"That," said Father, "is your problem. If you
made your bed properly every morning as Mother
tells you, this sort of thing wouldn't happen. I've
had a hard day, and I need a good night's sleep.
One more sound and I'll put you out for the bears
and the sabre-toothed tigers."

Littlenose started to say something, but Father

gave him a look. So he lay down again and pulled
the covers over his head. And, surprisingly, he
was soon fast asleep.

When Littlenose woke next morning Father had
already left for a day's hunting. Littlenose ate his
breakfast silently. He felt tired, and ached all over.
He said as much to Mother.

"It's your own fault," she said. "I shudder to
think of the state that bed of yours must be in. You
can spend this morning shaking and airing the
furs and making it up properly. Then you'll get a
good night's sleep—and Father will be in a better
frame of mind at breakfast."

Of course, a Neanderthal bed wasn't really a
bed as we know it. It was a pile of bear skins and
other furs which served both as mattress and
covers and was spread on the floor of the cave.
Littlenose had a special corner of his own, and he
began rather grumpily to drag his bedding out
into the middle of the cave. It was quite
remarkable what came to light, and even more
remarkable that he had managed to sleep at all.
There was an old flint knife and some lucky
coloured pebbles in the folds of one fur. Lifting up
another, an apple core and a couple of bones
tumbled out; the remains of a midnight snack. At

34

the very bottom of the heap a particularly hard lump was revealed as a spare fire-making flint, and a bad ache in Littlenose's side had obviously been the result of a discarded spear point. It was quite exciting. Like a treasure hunt. And Littlenose was beginning to develop a wonderful game when Mother said, "Right. Now get those furs outside and beat them until they are clean." And Littlenose found himself standing in a cloud of dust as he beat vigorously with a long, pliant stick at the furs lying across a rock. At length Mother was satisfied that the bedding was clean and fresh, and Littlenose wearily carried it back indoors. By the time he had spread it out in his own special corner he felt he wanted to lie down on it there and then and fall asleep. But instead he called to Two-Eyes, and together they made their way to Littlenose's favourite tree, where they did their more important thinking.

Leaning back against the trunk, Littlenose said, "You know, Two-Eyes, people are pretty unreasonable. Sleeping on the floor, I mean. It's all right for you. With your fur you could sleep on a clump of thistles all night without even noticing, but skin is a different matter entirely." And Littlenose rubbed gently at his ribs, which still carried an impression of the old flint knife and the lucky coloured pebbles. He leaned back and watched a bird disappear into the foliage above his head. "Now, birds have more sense," he said to Two-Eyes. "No lying on the hard ground for them. They build soft nests with wool and feathers

and things to line them. And I bet *they* never lose a single wink of sleep." He watched for the bird to reappear, and as he did so vague thoughts began to form in his mind. The thoughts became less and less vague the longer he considered them, until he suddenly leapt to his feet and shouted, "I've got it, Two-Eyes!"

Startled, Two-Eyes jumped sideways and gave Littlenose a suspicious look. He wasn't happy at all. Littlenose's ideas usually spelt trouble for someone—more often than not for Two-Eyes. He sneaked away as Littlenose paced up and down waving his arms as he explained his great idea.

"People nests!" he exclaimed. "If people had nests like the birds, there would be none of this business of hard floors. At bedtime they would simply snuggle down and be lulled to sleep by the gentle swaying of the branches." He was quite carried away, and only stopped when he ran out of breath. By which time Two-Eyes was nowhere to be seen. But Littlenose was not one to let a good idea grow cold. There and then he decided to build a "people nest", or rather a "boy nest", to prove that it could be done. "And when everyone sees what a good idea it is they'll all want them. I'll be the Tribal Nest Builder." But he wouldn't tell anyone. He'd been laughed at before. This time *he* would do the laughing.

From the sun Littlenose judged that it was almost lunch-time, but there was a lot he could do before then. He had to find a suitable tree, for instance. He set off into the woods.

Finding the right kind of tree turned out to be more difficult than Littlenose had imagined. To begin with, it had to be big enough for a boy-size nest. Then, as Littlenose couldn't fly like a bird, it had to be easy to climb. He was deep in the forest before he found what he was looking for. A tall, straight tree with plenty of hand and foot holds for climbing, and right at the top a stout limb growing straight out from the trunk with a large fork at the end. Littlenose wasted no time in scrambling up to have a closer look. It was perfect. Then he climbed back to the ground and started to gather twigs and branches for his nest. The time flew past, and Littlenose completely forgot that he should have been home for lunch. And when he did remember late in the afternoon, he thought, "No point worrying now. I'll be in trouble no matter when I go home." And he carried on dragging branches to the foot of the tree until he had a huge pile. Two-Eyes would have been handy for all this heaving and carrying, but Two-Eyes was wisely staying out of sight.

Now came the really tricky part; getting the branches to the top of the tree and building the nest. And tricky it certainly was. Littlenose could only carry one branch at a time as he climbed carefully to the fork. Soon his limbs ached and his hands were scratched and sore. The branches seemed to get heavier and heavier, but in the end the last one was up and carefully balanced with the others across the forked branch.

Having got this far, Littlenose was suddenly aware of a new problem. How was he going to fix it all together to make a nest? He had never considered for a moment how the birds managed it. He sat with his back to the tree-trunk and thought and thought. Then he took his flint knife out of his furs and carefully cut strips of bark about as long as his fore-arm and about as broad as his finger. Then he inched his way astride the branch and carefully began to arrange the nesting material across the fork, using the strips of bark to lash it firmly in place. It wasn't easy. He needed one hand to hold on with, and used the other hand and his teeth to tie the knots. But slowly the nest began to take shape. The gap in the forked branch became a platform of stout twigs, and Littlenose now began to weave and interlace the smaller pieces into the gaps. It was bowl-shaped and looking very nest-like, when he realised that he had run out of twigs. He didn't need many. Just enough leafy ones to make a soft and comfortable lining. He wouldn't even have to climb down to the ground either. He slid back along to the trunk and broke off all the leafy branches he could reach and threw them into the nest. Then he hung down and collected more from lower down. Then it was a simple matter to arrange them inside the woven branches—and the job was done. Littlenose looked at his handiwork with pride. Carefully he lay down on the soft leaves. It was bliss after all his hard work. He watched the clouds drift across the sky and a startled squirrel studying him from a safe distance. The nest rocked gently in the tree-top. And Littlenose fell asleep.

While Littlenose was putting the final touches to his boy-nest quite a lot was happening back at the caves. To begin with, when Littlenose didn't turn up at lunch-time, Mother was angry, but when there was still no sign of him at supper-time she became worried. For Littlenose to miss two meals in a row was most unusual. Mother asked around among the neighbours if they had seen Littlenose. But no one had. Then Father came home, and a full-scale search was mounted. This was quite a usual occurrence with the tribe. Hardly a week went by that Littlenose hadn't to be rescued from some predicament. With some reluctance and a lot of muttering the search party assembled in the gathering dusk.

"If that boy were mine," muttered one man, "I'd throw him to the bears."

"They'd throw him right back," said another. "Bears have more sense."

At length they were ready to leave. Father was just giving the order to march, when he stopped. There was a sound from the forest and a strange figure stumbled into the circle of torchlight. It was an old, old man. He carried a bundle of sticks in one shaking hand as he lurched and stumbled into the midst of the search party. He grabbed one man by the arm and wheezed and puffed, trying to speak and get his wind back at the same time.

"It's old Nod," said Father. "What on earth's the matter with him?" Nod was a simple old man who lived with his wife in a cave some way from the others. He spent most of his time collecting herbs

and running errands for his wife. He had evidently been gathering firewood in the forest.

After a moment Nod calmed down a bit and stopped gasping. Then he pointed dramatically back the way he had come and cried, "Big as a mammoth! Out of the sky! It'll have us all!"

"What will?" said Father.

"It!" cried Nod. And he darted about flapping his arms like wings and talking so fast that only one word in ten made sense. But a look of horror came over the faces of the search party as they

"You didn't believe all that nonsense?" said Father scornfully, and he started to laugh. But no one else laughed. In fact, there was complete silence. The moon had risen while they were speaking, and Father realised that the others were not even looking at him. They were gazing across a clearing, where a tall tree grew slightly separate from the rest. Their eyes travelled up the trunk. Up and up to where a large branch grew out near the top. And there they saw it.

There could be no doubt. It was a nest. But what

realised what Nod was telling them. He'd fled for his life from a giant bird! They asked questions. No, he hadn't actually *seen* a giant bird; but he *had* seen a giant nest. What more did they want?

"Could you lead us to it?" asked Father. Nod was perhaps simple, but he was far from stupid. Bringing news of a ferocious giant bird in the forest was one thing. Going back for a second look was something else altogether. He gathered up his firewood, bid them good night, and hurried off towards his cave. The men looked at each other. "Silly old man," said one. "Probably imagined the whole thing. Come on. We've wasted enough time as it is." And off they went on their delayed hunt for the missing Littlenose.

By the light of their torches the search party headed by Father picked their way cautiously through the forest. The moon had not yet risen, and outside the torchlight there were growls and rustles and occasional shining eyes as the night creatures went about their business. The men peered into the shadows, prodded the undergrowth with their spears, but of Littlenose there was no sign. They were deep in the forest when they paused to rest for a moment.

"Where can he be?" said Father.

"You don't suppose the giant bird got him?" said someone.

a nest. In the moonlight every twig stood out clearly, and at the thought of what had made it the search party drew back into the shadows. "What do we do now?" they asked each other.

Littlenose woke with a start. He hadn't meant to sleep, and now it was dark. He was really in trouble this time. The sooner he got home the better. He climbed out of his nest and slid along the branch to the trunk of the tree. He felt in the half light of the moon for foot and hand holds. And there were none! What had happened? Where were all the branches he had used to climb up? Then he remembered. The leafy branches he had broken off to make a comfortable lining. They were the same ones he had used to climb up. He was stuck. He got back into the nest, took a deep breath, and shouted with all his might: "HELP!"

To his amazement there was an immediate reply. A voice out of the darkness at the foot of the tree shouted, "Hi!" Then other voices joined in, including Father's. They were all talking at once. Mainly nonsense, by the sound. "It's Littlenose. It must have got him. It must be gigantic to carry him up there. Do you think he's all right? Are you all right, Littlenose?"

"Yes," cried Littlenose. "But I can't get down."

"He can't get down. Somebody will have to go up for him."

"Hang on, Littlenose," called Father. "I'll have you safe and sound in two shakes of a mammoth's tail." And slinging a coil of raw-hide rope on his shoulder, he began to climb the tree. He reached the last of the hand holds, balanced himself as best he could, and tied one end of the rope around his waist.

"Tie the end to the branch," he called to Littlenose, throwing the coiled rope towards him. Littlenose did this as tightly as he could, and waited to see what Father was going to do next. He never did find out, because at that moment Father, forgetting where he was, lost his balance and with a horrible yell vanished into the darkness. The search party scattered in all directions as Father plummeted towards them. But the rope had caught up in a great tangle and Father was brought up short halfway to the ground, where he dangled helplessly.

"Don't all just stand there," he cried. "Get me down." The men scratched their heads, looking up at him as he swung gently to and fro in the moonlight. One man had just climbed on to another's shoulders and was reaching up towards Father when a voice from overhead called down, "I'll get you down, Father."

Father twisted round and peered up to see what Littlenose was doing. "No!" he cried in horror. "Not that, Littlenose!"

Littlenose was clinging to the branch and sawing at the raw-hide rope with his flint knife. "Almost there," he called encouragingly, and before Father could utter another protest the rope parted. For the second time Father hurtled groundwards. He collided head-on with one of the search party. Luckily Neanderthal heads were made for rough treatment. Even as they tumbled in a heap, another body crashed amongst them. Relieved suddenly of Father's weight the branch along which Littlenose was lying had sprung suddenly upwards, catapulting him into the air.

The piled-up search party broke his fall safely, if a bit abruptly.

It took several moments for everyone to get his breath back. Then they painfully and stiffly got to their feet. They picked up the scattered torches and looked closely at Littlenose. "Look at those scratches," they said. "Must be claw marks. Or beak marks. What a dreadful experience." Littlenose hadn't a clue what they were talking about, and said nothing.

Then Father said, "We'd better not hang around here in case it comes back." The others nodded agreement, and the search party and Littlenose set off as fast as they could for home. All the way Littlenose expected to be scolded severely for staying out after dark, but instead everyone was extremely kind. They asked him strange questions which he answered as well as he could, until at last it dawned on Littlenose that there was an enormous misunderstanding somewhere. As he listened to the men's conversation it began to dawn on him. They thought that his boy nest had been built by a giant bird which had captured him. Well, well. He was even something of a hero. He wisely decided to say as little as possible and let them draw their own conclusions.

The whole tribe was gathered in front of the caves, and they cheered when they saw Littlenose safe and sound. Mother had tears in her eyes and Father wore a rather smug expression, evidently having forgiven Littlenose for cutting the rope. People even began to think that old Nod was perhaps not as simple as they had thought, and the whole tribe was convinced that Littlenose had had a very lucky escape.

Washed, fed and tucked up in bed by Mother, all Littlenose could think was that anyone who preferred a nest to a solid bed of bearskin must be positively bird-brained. With that thought he pulled the covers over his head, and in a moment was fast asleep.

PUZZLES

WHICH GADGET HAS'NT GOT A PLUG?

WHAT'S IN STORE?
EACH NUMBER'S A LETTER. READ THE LABELS AND FIND OUT.

① 18 9 3 5

④ 2,1,11,5,4 2,5,1,14,9

② 16,12,21,13 10,1,13

③ 7,9,14,7,5,18 19,14,1,16,9

⑤ 19,1,12,1,4 3,18,5,1,13
6,9,19,8

⑥ 6,9,14,7,5,18,19

HERE ARE THE NAMES OF SOME BBC TV PROGRAMMES. CAN YOU SPOT THEM?

① Y A L P A W Y A

② YAR AJO N KC

③ ARN TD GAS DN

④ SFE TTP HOOP PO

⑤ PRE OOUI HL MTD SOP CALWSU

⑥ DTA IINE ONW

⑦ OEAM TFHHD CTAY

⑧ OOOW TMRO RWSR DL

⑨ NR AP AOAM

⑩ CKA JRAC KECR

CAN YOU READ THIS MESSAGE?
JA CKAN DJI LLSB IRTHO AYW ASO
NS ATU RDA Y29 THJA NUA RY

WHO'S THE ODD MAN OUT?
THERE ARE PLAYERS FROM FIVE TEAMS HERE—BUT ONLY ONE FROM SCORELESS UNITED. WHICH IS HE?

RISING STARS

It's not often you come face to face with two Russian champions *and* a winner of five Olympic gold medals. But that's what happened to us when the biggest and best gymnastics squad ever to leave Russia arrived in Britain last autumn.

Fourteen-year-old Olga Koval was the youngest member of the Soviet National team that put on a stunning display of gymnastics and acrobatics at the Empire Pool, Wembley. Although she's still at school, Olga's already a World Cup Vault silver medallist as well as being a USSR Junior Champion. Her speciality is the beam, and you could have heard a pin drop in the crowded Blue Peter studio as we held our breath and watched her perform the most amazing contortions.

As Blue Peter is a "live" programme, there are no second chances, so it was really bad luck when Olga fell during her routine. But like a true professional, she jumped up and carried on. In a competition that slip would have lost valuable marks, but so far as we were concerned, Olga gained our admiration for the plucky way she kept her nerve.

Elena Davydova is a year older and has won particular praise for her floor exercises. So we filled the studio with an Olympic-sized mat and Elena performed the exercise that gained her the title of Junior Republican Champion of the USSR.

The manager of the team, and the girls' coach, is Larissa Latinina, who also has a string of gymnastic credits to her name, including no less than five Olympic gold medals!

Afterwards, Larissa, Olga and Elena talked in Russian about their gymnastics while an interpreter translated for us.

The message was unmistakable. To get to the top is sheer hard work, but that's what it takes to reach the heights of Nelli Kim and Nadia Comaneci—the only girls to get a 10 out of 10 mark in Olympic competition.

In 1980 Olga and Elena will probably be representing the USSR on their home ground, Moscow, and who knows, they may both become Olympic Champions!

Olga Koval's speciality is the beam.

Elena Davydova and her spectacular floor exercise.

Larissa Latinina, the girls' coach and Manager of Soviet National team, has won five gold medals.

BLUE PETER SPECIAL ASSIGNMENT

Thousands of towns in Britain have a "twin"—a town overseas which shares its interests and has a great deal in common. Pete and Lesley set off to France, Germany, Poland and Israel on the

TWIN TOWN TRAIL

1 Bordeaux; 2 Richmond; 3 Cambridge; 4 Heidelberg; 5 Fontainebleau; 6 Portsmouth; 7 Bristol; 8 Haifa. Do you know which towns are the twins? Answers on page 76.

A TALE OF TWO CITIES

These two cities are a thousand miles apart...

Warsaw is the capital of Poland in Eastern Europe. In winter it lies under deep snow, and the river Vistula, flowing through the town, is frozen. Coventry is in the heart of Britain's industrial Midlands and is famous for making cars.

The two cities are a thousand miles apart. What can they have in common?

Well, they both owe their beginning to a fairy-tale heroine who lived a thousand years ago.

Coventry's heroine is Lady Godiva. She was married to Leofric, Earl of Mercia and Lord of Coventry. He was a stern ruler who taxed his people unmercifully.

Godiva was gentle, beautiful and compassionate. She begged Leofric to spare the people, but he would not. At last, he told his wife that if she really wanted to make him believe she was ready to do anything for the people of Coventry, she would ride on her horse, naked, right through the town in broad daylight. At first she was horrified—then she sent messengers to tell the people she would do this for them if they would all stay in their houses. Then she let down her long, beautiful hair like a cloak all round her, mounted her horse and rode out into the silent town.

One man—the story goes—was overcome by temptation and looked through his window. But Peeping Tom was struck blind! Her task accomplished, Godiva returned joyfully to her husband, Leofric, who kept his promise and repealed the heavy taxes.

Warsaw's legendary lady is a mermaid! Long ago, she appeared from the waters of the river Vistula and told a group of startled fishermen that a great city would arise on the banks of the river. It would be founded by a man and a woman called Wars and Sawa, and would be known as Warsaw. She vanished again under the waves—but her prophecy came true!

After the help Leofric and Godiva gave to Coventry the town prospered. It became a rich trading city in the Middle Ages, and its greatest pride was its magnificent cathedral.

Coventry adapted to changing times, and a hundred years ago it became a modern industrial town. Bicycles, motor bikes and cars were all made

The symbol of Coventry. Lady Godiva, who was a champion of the people.

COVENTRY and WARSAW

.. both were destroyed but both rose up to live again.

The symbol of Warsaw. A mermaid who foretold the founding of the city.

n Coventry.

In 1596, King Sigismund of Poland moved his royal court from Cracow to Warsaw. Now Warsaw was the capital of the country, and it became one of the loveliest cities in Europe with a royal castle, an old town protected by huge walls, and a new town of wide, tree-lined avenues, palaces and parks where the nobility lived, and fine churches.

In 1939 these two cities, so unlike, and so far apart, both found themselves in the front line in the war against Hitler's Germany.

In the war years fighting equipment pouring out of Coventry's factories was vital to Britain's survival.

German bombers were ordered to put the whole town out of action and spread panic among the workers so that they would leave the city.

At ten minutes past seven on Thursday 14 November 1940 they struck. In that night of horror, 400 bombers in countless waves dropped 30,000 incendiary bombs, followed by 1000 high-explosive bombs, on Coventry.

Water mains were shattered, so fires blazed without restraint, though firemen fought heroically. Messengers, Civil Defence workers, anti-aircraft gunners carried on magnificently all night.

The All Clear sounded at 6.16 a.m., and in the grey, miserable dawn the people of Coventry surveyed their city.

Six hundred people had been killed—50,000 homes were damaged. Coventry's centre was a blackened ruin.

Worst of all, Coventry's glorious 500-year-old cathedral had been destroyed by fire. "All night long the city burned, and her cathedral burned with her," declared the cathedral's Provost.

Less than 48 hours later, King George VI came to show his sympathy with the stricken city. He stood amidst the cathedral ruins, and he found that a cross of charred wood had been set up on an altar made of rubble.

He found, too, a determined spirit to rebuild the cathedral. "The cathedral will rise again, more splendid than before," vowed the people of Coventry.

Another spirit, too, was stirring in their hearts.

Bablake—where people were first sent to Coventry.

Bicycles and motor cars made Coventry rich, famous, and a target for the enemy.

The old Cathedral was destroyed by enemy aircraft . . .

. . . and the new one was completed by an RAF helicopter.

COVENTRY

Perhaps for the first time the citizens of this self-contained industrial British town looked out from their own city. They saw a whole continent devastated by war, and all the nations of Europe fighting for freedom, and they thought of all the towns that had been bombed and had suffered like Coventry.

It was in the smouldering ruins of Coventry Cathedral that the Twin Town movement was born.

The town the Coventry people thought of most was Warsaw, for by then Warsaw was a byword for heroism and desperate resistance. German troops had poured across the country, and the Polish army could not stop them. Her allies were too far away to help.

Warsaw had been bombed, shelled and occupied by Nazi troops. The Germans threatened that Warsaw should only survive as a name in history, and they set to work to destroy the city, building by building, street by street.

Coventry chose a symbol for the rebirth of the city—it could have been a symbol for Warsaw, too. It was a cross of nails, made out of the ancient nails used to build the old cathedral, bound together by wire.

And Coventry itself was a symbol of the new world that would be rebuilt after the war.

Coventry decided to build a new cathedral—not a copy of the old one. The ruins were left as a memorial of the past, and beside them rose a new cathedral, beautiful in an entirely modern way.

The architect, Basil Spence, designed it, and craftsmen began work on the task of replacing a medieval cathedral in the twentieth century.

The day in 1962 when the new cathedral was consecrated in the presence of the Queen was a day of rejoicing for the whole country, and a triumph for Coventry.

Like Coventry, Warsaw emerged from the war a devastated, battle-scarred city, but the problems were different.

Coventry had been attacked in a single, appalling night of terror. Warsaw had known six grim years of Nazi occupation. At the end of the war 92% of the city of Warsaw was an expanse of rubble, and of the 1,300,000 people who used to live there 800,000 were dead.

Warsaw had become a ghost city.

Yet today Warsaw is once more a beautiful thriving place—not only are there fine modern buildings, but all the ancient glories of the city have returned. There are beautiful, Renaissance palaces, seventeenth-century churches and medieval houses.

Yet nothing is more than thirty years old.

To trace the almost unbelievable story of the rebirth of Warsaw, I went to visit one of the six men

Warsaw stood alone in the path of the Nazi forces.

ho stood in Warsaw's ashes and vowed to build
heir city for a second time.

He was not a great soldier, a war leader or a
politician, but a quiet and scholarly Professor of
archaeology at Warsaw University.

Professor Zachwatowicz was 28 years old when
the city fell. Now he is silver-haired and nearing 70,
but his eyes were full of fire when he told me the
fantastic story of the rebirth of Warsaw.

Every year, before the war, he used to set his
students a project of making a survey and taking the
exact measurements of the capital's important
historic buildings. When the Nazis declared they
would destroy every building in Warsaw, the
professor managed to get back to his old college. He
collected all the students' old exercise books and
exam papers, took them down to the cellars, and
built a wall to protect them.

After the barbaric destruction was over he crept
back, bribing the Germans on duty to let him get to
the ruins. He knocked down his wall, and there were
the papers—safe!

He smuggled them out of the city, and for months
they lay hidden in a small town fire station. Then,
when Warsaw was liberated at last and could be
rebuilt, all the plans were ready.

Warsaw could rise again from the ashes.

The people of Warsaw were not like the people of
Coventry. They did not want to make a new city,
they wanted their old city back again, in all its
splendour, just as it was before the Germans arrived,
so that future generations would see it as if the
Germans had never set foot there.

That is the task they set themselves—and that is
what they have achieved.

It is hard to believe as you walk through Warsaw
that *everything*—every avenue, every palace, every
church—was once in ruins and has been completely
rebuilt.

Some things in Warsaw are new. In the heart of the
city stands a memorial to the Heroes of Warsaw—to
all the men and women who fought for the city and
who died there.

Coventry has its own war memorial—it is the
Memorial Park, where a tree is planted for every
citizen of Coventry who died in the two world wars.

The memorials stand for the unconquerable spirit
of Coventry and Warsaw, the twin towns that are so
different, yet have shared so much.

Neither Coventry nor Warsaw wants to be
remembered for the misery and destruction war
brought to them.

They both want to be recognised as cities that
grove, if their citizens have strength and courage,
even in the face of the worst that can happen, the life
and greatness of the cities will endure.

A little shrine marks the spot where freedom fighters
were killed.

Today their grandchildren sing songs to their memory.

All Warsaw was destroyed, but today it stands exactly
as it used to be.

FLOUR CANDLES

Yes! I do mean flour!
There's nothing wrong with my
spelling. These flower candle
holders ARE flour—baked hard
as nails and painted. You can make
any flower you like, but I chose
holly to decorate a Christmas table.

Here's the recipe:
  4 dessertspoons of plain flour
  1 dessertspoon of salt
  2 dessertspoons of water
Mix it all together into a dough
and you're ready to start. This is what to do:

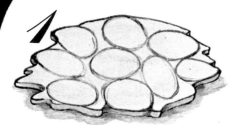

LEAVES

Flatten out the dough on a floured board and cut it into rough leaf shapes. I got nine out of my lump, which left a couple of spares in case of accidents!

When the leaves are cold, paint them with shiny green enamel and leave them to dry. A good tip when you paint the berries shiny red is to stick them into a lump of plasticine.

LINE WITH PLASTICINE TO HOLD CANDLE FIRMLY

METAL TOP COVERED WITH FOIL AND GLUED TO BASE

CARD COVERED WITH GOLD FOIL

Using the tip of a spoon, nip out the holly "prickles" and mark the leaf veins on with the point of a knife. Keep all the left-over bits of dough and roll into holly berries.

THE BASE

While the paint dries, make the base. Using a round lid as a pattern, cut out a circle of card. Glue on shiny foil to cover the card and fold and stick down the edges to neaten them. Cover a metal bottle top with foil and glue it into the centre. Make sure it is *metal*. Plastic could melt or even catch fire—so don't use it.

Push the berries on to each end of a bit of fuse wire and put them together with the leaves on a baking tray. Cook for several hours at a low temperature until hard and dry. If you can, put them in when a casserole stew is being cooked. That's ideal—and saves fuel, too! Look at them from time to time, and if they're puffing up, poke them flat again with a spoon. Gently, mind!

Arrange the leaves round the candle holder and glue them into place. You can either leave the berries on the wire stalks and twist them into the leaves—or take them off and glue them straight on to the base. Either looks nice, so it's up to you!

Put your bathing trunks on before you leave home.
This is one of the unbreakable rules for competitors in

THE GLEN NEVIS RIVER RACE

Of course, I obeyed the instructions, but I didn't discover the reason until a few moments before the race began.

In fact, I very nearly missed this extraordinary sporting event altogether. A letter came to the Blue Peter office in the spring inviting me to Scotland to take part in the annual river race with the Lochaber Mountain Rescue team. I had to turn it down because the dates clashed with the Blue Peter summer filming expedition. But I didn't get away with it that easily!

A letter came winging back saying "Tell us when you're free and we'll put on a special race for you." With an offer like that, who could refuse? So on 17 September when the temperature in the glen was about 5 degrees centigrade, I packed my wet suit and set off for the Highlands.

I was met by Neil Ewell, one of the founders of the race and a member of the Lochaber Mountain Rescue Team.

The River Race was dreamed up by the team as an idea to raise money to buy equipment which enables them to rescue climbers who are trapped on mountain ledges, or who may have fallen into deep crevices. Last year, the team—all volunteers—turned out on 34 rescues and spent 710 hours on the mountainside, mostly in appalling weather conditions. There are many people who wouldn't be alive today if it wasn't for the men of the Lochaber Mountain Rescue Team.

Neil took me on a tour of the two-mile course so that I could see what I was in for before the race began. It runs down the crags formed by the cataracts that sweep down from snow-capped Ben Nevis, the tallest mountain in Britain.

Neil had a gentle Highland voice that takes the drama out of everything.

"This section here, John," he said, pointing to a foaming mass of white water, "is called the 'gurgle'."

"Why's that?" I said—and regretted it straight away.

"Well, you tend to spend more time under the water than you do on top of it!"

"And this bit?" I asked as we looked at another torrent, but this time broken up by huge, jagged boulders.

"We call that the 'leg breaker'," he said.

This time I didn't make any comment.

It would have been bad enough in a canoe where you can hope to spend some of the time in the dry, but the Glen Nevis River Race is for men—or women—and AIR BEDS!

We were due to report at one o'clock for briefing. A large crowd had gathered to watch the start and there were knots of spectators clustered at the most hazardous sections of the course. As I looked round at the crowd, it dawned on me why I'd been told to put my trunks on before leaving the hotel. Changing into a wet suit before a crowd of spectators could prove to be a trifle embarrassing!

I put on a pair of baseball boots to protect my feet from the jagged rocks, and a crash helmet to

I joined Alan Kellock and Neil Ewell to be briefed on how to shoot down Glen Nevis on an air bed.

The first section is called the "gurgle" where you spend more time underneath the water than on top.

The next is called "leg breaker". This time I didn't ask why.

49

do the same for my head. Then I picked up my air bed, and looking like a right Charlie, I joined the others for the start.

In the summer race with 50 competitors, there are two-minute delays between each person to prevent a total shambles at the beginning. Today as there were only six of us, the delays were cut down to ten seconds. We all drew a number out of a hat, got into line, and waited for the command to enter the water. I drew number three, so it wasn't long before the starter, Jim Leslie, looking very splendid in a deer-stalker hat, clicked his stopwatch and called "Number 3—OFF!"

The cold when I hit the water was beyond belief. Without our wet suits we would surely have died in the first hundred metres. It wasn't too rough at the very beginning, but swift enough for me to discover that when you're lying on an air bed you can't see what's coming until just before you hit it.

The "gurgle" was something else. The odd moments when I broke the surface and felt the incredible strength of the current hurling me

I paddled my way limply towards the finishing post.

down the gorge were as exhilarating as the "Cresta Run". But most of the time I was fighting for my breath as I was dragged beneath the water, clinging on to my air bed for dear life.

"Leg breaker" was like a nightmare with huge, black boulders being flung at you by a mad, maniac monster.

Then suddenly I was into smooth-flowing deep water, but there was no time to rest. I had to paddle like fury with my hands to stay in the race.

I could hear an ominous roar ahead of me and through the foam I could see a man frantically waving me in to the bank. I climbed ashore and asked him what was the matter.

"You can't go on," he shouted at me. "There's a big waterfall ahead. Follow the markers along the bank and they'll show you where to get back in."

When I started to walk I discovered that I had no power at all in my legs. I staggered and weaved my way along the markers until I saw a large crowd of people leaning over a bridge. The roar of the waterfall had increased and then I noticed the figure of Neil standing still just ahead of me. I tried to shout above the torrent—and then suddenly he disappeared. I ran down to where he had been standing and discovered the awful truth. 10 clear metres—30 feet below me was the foot of the falls—and bobbing about on the water was a tiny red blob that must have been Neil swimming towards his air bed.

"Don't worry," said a steward, "there's a diver in the water in case you get into trouble."

"Thanks a bundle," I said. "I'm *always* in trouble."

I remember Butch Cassidy saying to the Sundance Kid in similar circumstances: "It's not the fall that kills you, it's the sudden stop at the bottom."

There's one thing to be said about jumping—all you need is the courage to step off—after that, there's no turning back.

You go down quite a long way when you hit the water from a 10-metre drop wearing baseball boots, a wet suit and crash helmet. I'd no idea where my air bed was. My thoughts, if I had any, were concentrated on getting to the top before a lung exploded. I was deafened by the waterfall as soon as I broke the surface, and there, to my everlasting relief and delight, I saw one of the Fort William Sub-Aqua Club divers giving me a cheery wave as he pushed my air bed towards me.

By the time I reached the finishing post I was absolutely exhausted. None of us really knew or cared who'd won. We just bobbed about, giggling in the water, too tired even to make the effort to climb out of the river.

The incredible toughness and dedication of the Lochaber Mountain Rescue team amazed me. Every year they put on this gruelling race to entertain the holidaymakers. The money they collect from the tourists is used to equip the team to rescue the tourists who get into trouble on the mountain. It takes all sorts, I thought, as I peeled off my wet suit—and these guys must be some of the best.

In the end, I was too exhausted even to climb out of the water.

From a grocery carton, some cardboard tubes and some egg boxes, you can make a game that all the family can play. It's cheap and it's fun, and if you make it carefully, it should last for ages. Here's what to do.

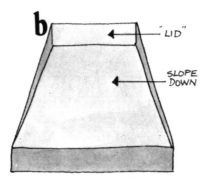

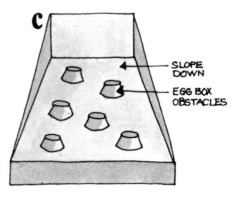

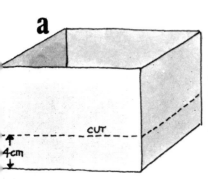

1 THE BASE

a) Mark a line about 4 cms from the bottom of a grocery carton and cut carefully. When you've finished it will look like a lid.

b) From one of the left-over sides, cut a piece of card the same size as the "lid". Glue it in place to make a slope. One short side should fit into the bottom of the "lid" and the other should rest on the edge. It's down this slope that the marbles will run.

c) To make the game more fun, you'll need some obstacles. Make these from egg boxes. Cut out the egg sections and, using just a dab of glue, put them roughly in place. Roll a marble down the slope to make sure it will hit the obstacles and not run straight through. When you're satisfied, glue the egg sections firmly in place. Don't make the run too easy!
Paint the finished base all over with emulsion paint. For extra strength, a top coat of gloss is a good idea.

2 THE TOWERS

a) Make towers from cardboard tubes from kitchen towel or toilet rolls. You'll need four about 4 cms high, and one a bit taller. In each one, cut an arch for a marble to get through. Paint the towers, and when they're dry, draw in the stonework with a black felt-tipped pen.

b) Glue the small towers in a row at the bottom of the slope. Cut the bottom of the tall tower at an angle to match the slope and glue in place at the top.

3 FLAGS & RULES

Cut out scoring flags from paper or sticky-backed plastic stuck on to cocktail or match sticks and glue in place at the top of the small towers.

To play the game, drop a marble down the big tower and try to get it into a scoring tower. Add up the points as you go along. In our rules,

the winner is the one who gets the most points in six throws, but you can make up your own. Hope you enjoy it. We do!

53

WHISKER LICKIN' GOOD!

On Monday 31 January at about three minutes past five Jack and Jill tucked into their very first birthday cake.

They had a high old time at their party, and both of them (Jill especially) were fascinated with the eye-catching cards you sent them.

The birthday tea was a great success. The hosts sat on the table and when the cake was brought on the guests had their cold noses stuck in the chicken-flavoured icing in no time!

Here are some souvenir pictures of the twins' First Birthday Party.

THE CASE OF THE TANGLED TAPE

CHAMPIONSHIPS

In the glare of the spotlights, Igor and Irene executed a faultless double axel, and to a tumultuous round of applause they skated off the rink to await the results of the finals of the International Schools Pairs Skating Championships.

"Gosh," whispered Bob to his friends, Liz and Phil, "that Transylvanian pair are going to take some beating, but I know you can do it!"

It was an exciting moment for Bob when he was picked to accompany his class-mates to represent Britain at the Schools Championships. The three friends had flown out to the Italian Alps with Bob's uncle, Detective Inspector McCann, who was in charge of security for the whole championships, and so far they'd all been having a marvellous trip. Bob was anxious to do everything he could to make things smoother for Liz and Phil off the ice so that they could concentrate on their performance.

The three from England had soon made friends with Igor and Irene. They were easy to get on with, and spoke very good English. Their chaperon, though, was a very different matter. He was a Transylvanian official called Ricardo Kaustovich. He was on his way to a job at the Embassy and had offered to accompany the pair as travelling companion. Neither Igor nor Irene had met him until they got on the plane!

"He's no fun," moaned Irene, "but we're told he's a retired skating judge, so he should be able to give us some hints to help our performance!"

Now the competition was in progress, Igor and Irene looked better than ever, and the three friends watched breathlessly as the marks flashed on the electronic scoreboard.

"5.6, 5.6," breathed Liz, "and one 5.9." She turned to Phil and Bob. "Do you think we've got a chance?"

"Of course you have!" cried Bob. "Just wait till

hey see your routine to 'Greensleeves' and that running change into 'Hard Day's Night'. Tomorrow, when it's your turn, you just show them! You two go off and get a good rest, and I'll take the music tape up now so it's all ready for the morning.''

As Phil and Liz went back to the hotel, Bob made his way up to the sound control room high above the rink. Giorgio Agerossi, the Sound Supervisor, glanced up as Bob peered round the door.

"Ciao," he said. "You bring de musica for de inglese?"

"Yes," said Bob.

"Leave it on de deska. I will take care of everythink!"

"Thanks," said Bob, his eyes glancing over the sophisticated equipment. "That's a marvellous tape deck you've got there! Is it difficult to operate?"

"No, no," explained Giorgio. "So longa as de green light is on, I know everythink's OK!"

The door creaked open and Ricardo Kaustovich, the Transylvanian official, appeared.

"We'll see about that in the morning," said Bob.

"He's not very friendly," thought Bob as he slipped away. "Still, Liz and Phil will give him something to worry about."

As he climbed down the steep stairs, he could hear the Transylvanian's surly reply to Giorgio's cheerful "Goodnight", and his heavy footsteps grow nearer. Bob hurried so that he wouldn't have to walk back to the hotel with him.

In the empty control box Giorgio settled down to his supper. He unwrapped his rolls and salami, opened his Chianti bottle and poured himself a glass of red wine. As he sipped, his eyes glanced down at the tape deck.

"Mama mia! The green light's out! I must get this fixed before the morning!" And he darted out to his workshop, leaving his meal uneaten.

The following day Bob took his seat next to his uncle and watched nervously as Liz and Phil stood out in the centre of the rink waiting for the music to start which would herald their bid for the International Schools Championship. As the first notes of "Greensleeves" echoed round the stadium, Bob breathed a silent "Good luck" as the graceful pair began their routine.

"Is this where I bring the tapes for tomorrow?" he asked.

"You're on the same job as me," grinned Bob. "I've just brought *our* team's tape," he said, nodding towards the sound desk.

"Is that the British tape?" he asked.

"It certainly is," said Bob, cheerfully.

The Transylvanian's eyes narrowed. "You're wasting your time," he grunted. "You don't stand a chance."

"Off to a good start, eh, Bob!" smiled Detective Inspector McCann. One perfect figure followed another, and Bob felt sure they were in with a very big chance. There was a flurry of ice as Liz and Phil waited for the music to change for their spectacular finale to the Beatles' number. Then something happened!

Panic seized the British pair! Instead of "Hard Day's Night", the strident notes of massed bagpipes screeched across the arena! With stumbling steps, they tried to fit their routine to the music, but it was hopeless. Liz and Phil skated off the ice, and over the tannoy came a dreadful announcement—"The

British pair have been disqualified for leaving the rink''.

* * *

Thirty minutes later McCann called a conference in the sound control room to discover what had gone wrong. Present were a distraught Bob, Giorgio—who was beside himself with horror at what had happened—Liz, Phil—and the Transylvanian representative, Ricardo Kaustovich, who had been hastily summoned from the middle of a conference in the town.

"The judges' decision is final,'' he snapped. "Even though I wasn't here to see what occurred, for the sake of international relations we must accept it. Transylvania is the undoubted winner.''

"Nevertheless, sir,'' declared Detective Inspector McCann, "we must discover what happened.''

"Now, Bob,'' he turned to his ashen-faced nephew, "you insist that you gave the tape to Giorgio?''

"Si, si, signor,'' confirmed the Italian. "He put it on the desk and no one touched it again until I played it this morning.''

"So, young man,'' sneered Kaustovich, "you are responsible. *You* have caused the downfall of your compatriots with those hideous bagpipes!''

"No, I didn't,'' said Bob, desperately. "Come to think of it, you saw me hand the tape over yourself!''

"Is that right, sir?'' queried McCann.

"Si, si, signor,'' interpolated Giorgio. "This gentleman brought his tape at the same time—and no one else could have come in or I would have noticed.''

"So you never left the tapes for a moment, then?'' asked McCann.

"Well, just for a minute when I noticed a fault in the tape deck and went to get my tools,'' admitted a sheepish Giorgio.

"Such slipshod maintenance would not be tolerated in Transylvania!'' snarled Kaustovich.

Poor Giorgio protested: "But, signor, I do my best. I take great care!''

Kaustovich silenced him.

"You drink too much. If you had paid more attention last night instead of pouring red wine down your throat and stuffing yourself with salami, you might not have ruined the competition!''

"Has this kind of thing ever happened before, in your experience?'' McCann asked Kaustovich.

"Not that I remember,'' he replied. "When I was judging at the Winter Olympics last year, at Aviemore, the atmosphere was delightful and the Scots so efficient.''

"You enjoyed your trip, then?'' smiled McCann.

"Yes—everything about it!'' For once, the Transylvanian was transported as his mind went back to Scotland. "There was the beautiful setting,'' he mused, "with the rink at the foot of the Pennines, and most unforgettable, the applause as your champion, John Curry, won the pairs skating with that sensational score of 9.8! I shall never forget it!''

"And I don't think you'll forget *this* championship, either,'' rasped McCann, as suddenly he snapped the handcuffs on the Transylvanian.

"Eh, what . . .'' gasped Bob, turning to a startled Liz and Phil.

"Ricardo Kaustovich has made six very foolish slips,'' triumphed McCann, "which should keep him on ice for a very long time.''

Did you spot the six mistakes? Check your answers on page 76.

58

Finders Keepers

0-year-old Gary Fridd of Gilling West will never forget the day he was looking for tadpoles in the stream near his home. When he spotted a glint of metal and bent down to investigate, he picked up a sword that had once belonged to an Anglo-Saxon warrior!

Considering the sword is one thousand one hundred years old, it's in remarkable condition. We could hardly believe our eyes when Gary brought it to the studio and we felt the weight of it. It's solid silver and iron, with a hilt decorated with fine silver bands and a blood-thirsty, 81-centimetre-long blade.

Because the workmanship is so good, the sword probably belonged to a Chieftain and not an ordinary soldier. And experts think peat at the bottom of the stream protected it from serious decay during the eleven hundred years it was lost.

But Gary had to fight to keep his sword. You can't just hang on to treasures you find lying about. First, he had to go to court, where a jury sat to decide whether or not the sword was "Treasure Trove". If it *was*, it was Crown property. But Gary was in luck.

The jury decided the sword had been abandoned and that it *wasn't* Treasure Trove, and he was allowed to keep it. But the battle wasn't over. A few weeks later the trustees of the estate where the sword was found claimed that Gary had been trespassing and threatened a High Court action to get it back. Then, just when it looked as though all was lost, one of the trustees, Lord Bolton, who'd been away and knew nothing about the court case, stepped in and said *he* wanted Gary to keep his find. The others agreed, and the action was dropped. And on 20 April, at Christie's, the sword was auctioned for a staggering £10,000! It's been bought by the Yorkshire Museum at York, so it's saved for the nation for everyone to see. And it'll be worth seeing, too. Gary's sword is in far better condition than the only other one of its kind. The Fiskerton sword at the Sheffield Museum is so fragile it can't be moved.

As for Gary, he's going to buy a bike and put the rest of the money in the bank. He says he'll keep his eyes skinned the next time he goes tadpole hunting—for, who knows, there may be even more treasure under the water at Gilling Beck.

BE MY VALENTINE-AND EAT IT!

You wouldn't think that three old bananas could turn into a mouth-watering cake *and* four sumptuous party trifles. But that's what happens with my New Zealand Banana Cake recipe. The basic mixture is delicious in itself. But with a bit of imagination you can transform it into a special St Valentine's cake—and nothing's wasted! The bits you trim off to make the heart shape can be used as a basis for banana trifles. Why not send a Valentine with a difference next February 14th—an edible one.

BANANA CAKE

Ingredients:

3 bananas (old ones are best)
4 oz (113 g) butter
4 oz (113 g) sugar
6 oz (171 g) self-raising flour

2 tablespoons of milk
1 teaspoon of bicarbonate of soda
2 eggs

1 Cream together the butter and sugar.

2 Mash the bananas and mix them into the butter and sugar.

3 Beat the eggs in another bowl, then beat into the mixture.

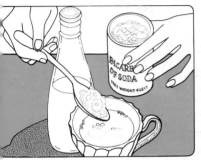

4 Put the milk in a cup and stir in the bicarbonate of soda.

5 Mix the flour and the milk into the main mixture, about a third at a time and alternating between the two.

6 Put the mixture into a greased cake tin (a square one if you want a heart shape) and cook for 45 minutes at Gas Mark 4, or 350°F. or 180°C. After 45 minutes you should be able to push a skewer into the centre of the cake and pull it out with *no* mixture sticking to it. If necesary cook a little longer.

BANANA TRIFLE

The crumbs left over from trimming the cake to a heart shape can be used for individual trifles by adding custard, instant whip, or jelly, and topping with cream and slices of fresh banana.

DECORATION

For a Valentine cake, bake in a square tin and cut the heart shape like this:

Cover with butter icing (creamed butter and icing sugar) or lemon icing—icing sugar mixed with lemon juice or lemon squash. Decorate with cherries, chocolate flakes, hundreds and thousands and silver balls.

SAVE THE CRUMBS

For the trifles.

Mystery Picture

0	Leave white
1	Pink
2	Deep purple
3	Yellow
4	Orange
5	Blue
6	Red
7	Green
8	Dark green

Colour the spaces as indicated by the numbers and the mystery picture will appear.

THE KING'S APPENDIX
<<<<<

This magnificent teapot is a souvenir of the Coronation of King Edward VII—but have you spotted the mistake?

A curious story lies behind not only the teapot, but hundreds of other commemorative souvenirs of the Coronation of 1902.

On 22 January 1901 the aged Queen Victoria had died at Osborne. Her son, Albert Edward, the Prince of Wales, whom his family called "Bertie", was the next King, and he declared he wished to be known as King Edward VII.

The new King was fifty-nine years old, so he had waited a long time to come to the throne. Plans for the Coronation were put in hand, and a date was fixed—26 June 1902. Because Queen Victoria had taken little part in State Ceremonial for many years, this Coronation was to be a splendid occasion. It was to mark the beginning of a new reign, *and* a new century, so the souvenir makers got busy. They made mugs and medals, plates, jugs and teapots—all marked with the Coronation date—26 June 1902.

As the day drew near, Westminster Abbey was made ready, decorations went up in streets all over London, and sightseers flocked to the capital. Foreign VIPs began to arrive—royalty from all nations—all ready and waiting for the Coronation.

The new King plunged into the arrangements with great gusto, so when, early in June, he began to feel unwell, he just thought he was overtired. He tried to

Queen Victoria died in January 1901.

The next year the streets were decorated to celebrate her son's Coronation—planned for 26 June.

Would the King recover? Crowds flocked to Buckingham Palace for the latest news.

9 August 1902 was the date of the real Coronation, but many souvenirs were dated 26 June.

rest, but only felt worse and worse. Then his doctors examined him and diagnosed—appendicitis!

In those days not much was known about appendicitis, and an operation for it was very rare. Everyone was desperately worried about the Coronation, and the King's doctor tried to keep the newspapers quiet by telling them the King had lumbago.

But the King said he was determined he would attend his Coronation, even if he dropped dead during the long service.

He went to Buckingham Palace, and there, on 23 June—three days to go—his doctors examined him again. They told him he was seriously ill and *must* be operated on at once. They said they had secretly prepared a room in Buckingham Palace as an operating theatre, and that the Coronation must be postponed indefinitely! King Edward replied angrily that he would not disappoint his subjects—but he was so ill he *had* to give way.

The next day—24 June—the operation was carried out successfully. People flocked to Buckingham Palace to wait for the latest news. A special "Service of Intercession" with prayers for the King's recovery was held in St Paul's Cathedral, and a public announcement was made declaring the postponement of the Coronation.

Fortunately, the King began to get better. He went away on convalescence and then came back to London. A new Coronation Day was fixed—9 August 1902, and that was when the King was at last crowned King Edward VII in Westminster Abbey, and when he paraded through the streets of London in his Coronation procession the crowds went wild! At last they'd been able to celebrate, and they bought their Coronation souvenirs in their thousands—even though some of them *did* have the wrong date. And now, of course, they're extremely interesting collectors' items.

If *you've* got an Edward VII souvenir with the wrong date, you'll find it's becoming increasingly valuable—thanks to the royal appendix!

JUBILEE!

Blue Peter viewers had a chance to make a very special contribution to Queen Elizabeth I's Silver Jubilee Celebrations when we asked you to paint a commemorative picture for the Jubilee issue of the *Radio Times*.

Out of more than 65,000 entries, the top prize-winning picture chosen by the judges, including Art Editor David Driver, was by five-year-old Nicola Griffin of Camberley. And Nicola scored a double first with her patriotic guardsman with his flag and flowers. She was the first Blue Peter viewer and the first five-year-old in the world ever to design a *Radio Times* cover.

Cover girl Nicola! Out of the nine Top Prize Winners in our competition, Art Editor David Driver helped us choose her guardsman for the Jubilee *Radio Times*.

BLEEP & BOOSTER

A stellar[] advent[] in outer space

It was Exploding Stars Night. In a couple of hours' time the sky over Miron City would be alight with a dazzling display of meteorites, bursting in a shower of gold and silver as they hit the planet's atmosphere and exploded.

The meteorites were positive electrons and broke up as soon as they touched anything. They could destroy a space freighter easily—but with the air fleet grounded there was no danger and as a further precaution there was an unmanned Fragmentiser satellite in orbit over the city. It acted as a sort of decoy duck, attracting any unexploded meteorites and disintegrating them high above the city.

The planet Miron only passed through the positive electronite belt once in five years. To celebrate, Bleep was giving an Exploding Stars Night Party for the Space cubs. No wonder they were all agog—except Booster! He'd got something on his mind.

With a final flourish, Bleep spread the last dollop of stellarcream and peppered the top of his star-shaped cake wih shiny Gravity Balls. He stoo[] back, triumphant.

"There," he said to Booster. "All my own work! What do you think of it?"

It was magnificent, Booster thought, and normally he would have said so. But today he wa[] in a thoroughly bad mood.

"It's OK," he said in an off-hand way, and then wished he'd said something nicer when Bleep's face went pale green with disappointment.

After weeks of work, Booster's newest gadget was ready to test. He had worked out how to power his space scooter on Energon. It was Miron's greatest treasure—a fuel so powerful tha[] enemy planets were constantly trying to steal it—especially the creatures from Grimus. It was when Bleep and Booster had helped to confound a Grimaloid plot to occupy the Energon field that Booster had taken a lump as a souvenir. There was a strict Miron rule that Energon should never leave the planet, but no one would notice a tiny bit in his scooter, he decided, and for months he'd been redesigning its engine to cope with the new fuel.

In theory, it should treble its power and speed—but would it? And now, just when he was ready for the first test flight, all space craft

were grounded!

The party wasn't happening for ages, so to pass the time Booster switched on the television set. It was Moonday, and he'd been looking forward all week to seeing the last episode of *The Perilous Planet*. Would Captain Streak and his glamorous mauve assistant, Whirly Girl, escape from the Stentaurs?

Booster could hardly wait to find out.

"Here, Bleep," he cried, giving the set a thump, "what's the matter with this? It's gone all misty!"

"Of course it has," said Bleep. "Miron's only a few thousand miles now from the Positive Electronite Belt. It causes so much radio interference there'll be no telly tonight—and no radio, no phones, nothing!"

At that moment the screen went blank. So did Booster's face! No scooter test, no telly—and hours to wait for the big display! He was absolutely fed up, and although Bleep had been pretty annoyed that Booster hadn't done a thing

to help with the party, he felt quite sorry for him. After all, he hadn't taken much interest in Booster's invention, either!

"Here," he said, "let's have a look at that scooter thing of yours. What's so special about it?"

Proudly, Booster showed it to Bleep. "It'll practically run forever," he said. "We won't have to keep coming back for more fuel just when we're starting to get somewhere interesting!"

"Stellarific!" said Bleep. "How many bottles of asteroidade do you think we're going to need?"

"Never mind about that now!" said Booster. "Look, I know space flights are cancelled, but if we hurry we've just got time to test the scooter before Miron goes into the Positive Electronite Belt." And since Bleep looked more than a bit doubtful, he added hastily—"As soon as we get back, I'll help with the party, really!"

"Done!" cried Bleep, though he felt a bit guilty as he helped his friend manoeuvre the scooter outside. He hadn't told his father, the Captain, where they were going and for a good reason. He knew he'd say "No!" Still, they were only going to be a few minutes and as Booster blasted off and they shot spacewards faster than ever before, Bleep too was full of excitement!

*   *   *

It was strange, out in space, not being able to hear Miron Control on the radio, or join in any of the conversations between the people on hundreds of spaceships that usually went on all the time. Bleep had to be specially careful navigating to keep away from the belt of Positive Electronite that they could see spread across Miron's path around the sun. As Booster accelerated and braked and looped the loop, trying out all the controls and feeling how fast and powerful the new engine was, there was no one else in the whole sky to disturb them. For almost the first time in his life, Bleep felt lonely in space. As he glanced upwards he could see in the far distance tiny stars appearing and disappearing. The first of the meteorites were beginning to explode! Bleep knew that if they hung around they'd soon be surrounded with whizzing chunks of white-hot rock.

"Let's go, Booster!" he yelled.

Instantly, Booster swung the scooter round, and that moment something startling happened! Amidst the white light, they became aware of a dark shape. Somewhere up there a strange spaceship loomed, circling and wheeling in a curious way!

"It's the Fragmentiser satellite," cried Bleep. "But it's supposed to be in a stationary orbit. It must be out of control! We've got to get to it!"

Booster was aghast. "But it's right inside the Positive Electronite Belt," he gasped. "And it's too far away! I don't know if my Energon engine is good enough!"

"Look, Booster," said Bleep, desperately, "we've got to try. If that Fragmentiser isn't *exactly* on course, there'll be nothing to deflect the meteorites. They'll crash into Miron City like bombs—

just think of the crowds waiting for Exploding Stars Night! They'll be smashed to bits!''

Without a word, Booster gave the scooter all the power he could. At lightning speed they reached the satellite unscathed, thanks to Bleep's careful navigation, and found the outside landing platform. As they stopped, Booster glanced at the fuel gauge—it was all right! The Energon was holding out!

As they peered through the porthole in the airlock, Bleep and Booster were horrified. Inside

the supposedly unmanned Fragmentiser shadowy figures moved! Scaly arms manipulated the controls and beaky faces were glued to the instrument panels. Bleep and Booster clutched each other in fright! Grimaloids!

Booster was baffled.

"What are they doing here, Bleep?" he cried. "What can they want with a patched-up Fragmentiser all burned up and dented with exploding meteorites?"

"Can't you see," sobbed Bleep. "They'll take it back to Grimus. Miron City will have no protection from the stray meteorites. It will be devastated and then the Grimaloids will invade and steal our Energon! Oh, Booster, what shall we do?"

Before they had time to think of a plan there was a frightening hiss—the air lock opened and leathery arms grabbed them, scooter and all, and dragged them inside. With an echoing clang, the air lock closed behind them. They were trapped!

Quickly Bleep and Booster summed up the

position.

"Four of them," whispered Bleep, "and two of us. We haven't much chance, have we?" and a small, green tear rolled down his cheek.

"Two of us," replied Booster, "and Energon! Hang on, this is going to be a rough ride!"

Snapping the controls to full power, and with Bleep clinging on behind, Booster flung his scooter round the cabin like a hideous scythe. Grimaloids leapt from its path—scattering in all directions. Booster bounced the scooter off the bulkheads recklessly. Anything was better than being prisoners of the Grimaloids, and as he skidded across the instrument panel he caught one crack in the beak! It was too much for the Grimaloids. One flung open the air lock and within seconds they'd all jumped out into space, rapidly spinning away out of sight. Bleep and Booster were safe!

After the roar of the engines it was deathly quiet in the cabin. Just a faint hum came from the Fragmentiser's jets, and an occasional explosion as yet another stray meteorite burst against the dented hull.

Booster hardly noticed, but Bleep had a grave

ook on his face. He was busy checking the instruments, and as Booster looked at his friend he knew he'd discovered something bad!

CRASH! Another meteor exploded against the side, and Bleep turned to Booster desperately.

"You've bust the Fragmentising beam with your bike," he cried. "Meteorites aren't supposed to blow *us* to bits. The satellite's supposed to blast *them*, but you've cracked the fuel supply pipe. It won't work and we'll be blown to smithereens! Here, how much fuel have you got left? Let's get out of here!"

Rapidly Booster checked.

"Enough to get back," he said, "but this is the only fuel we've got. And we *can't* use it. It's needed here."

Stupefied, Bleep watched as his friend began to dismantle the scooter. "We'll die here," he cried, as another deafening crash rocked the satellite. "What are you doing?"

"We need the Energon power cells," snapped Booster. "Quick, give me a hand."

Within seconds Booster had them connected to the fuel lines of the Fragmentising beam and Bleep was happily exploding stray meteorites as they approached.

"You've saved the satellite, and you've saved Miron City, Booster," he cried. "You have broken the rules, but it seems to me Energon in space has a great future. What are you going to save next?"

"Your Exploding Stars Night Party," he laughed. "They can't cut the cake without you, so let's get rescued! Here, give me a go on the Fragmentising beam! There may be no radio contact, but now we're manually controlled it's easy enough to send a signal! I'll explode ten asteroids into a code!"

The Captain was worried when Bleep and Booster were still missing as Miron entered the asteroid belt. He'd guessed what had happened when he found the scooter missing, but he hoped they'd got enough sense to take refuge on another planet until it was safe to come back to Miron. He told Space Traffic Control, and then went home to try and look after all the guests that

Bleep had invited to the party, though he himself wouldn't enjoy it at all, knowing that the boys might be in danger. Now everyone was picnicking in the open air, watching the sky. There had been no more than a couple of flashes, when suddenly a whole string of meteorites exploded across the sky in showers of golden rain—short short long—short short long—short short long—and after that a more complicated message that the Captain read with a wider and wider smile spreading across his face.

* * *

With Bleep clearing a path through the positive electronite field for the Space Commando's rescue ship, the Captain arrived safely. He re-set the Fragmentising beam to automatic, and now all three of them were heading for home.

"You shouldn't have taken the Energon, Booster," the Captain said, "but the way things turned out, I'm glad you did."

"Yes," laughed Bleep, "your super scooter turned out to be a real life saver! Captain Streak and the Whirly Girl couldn't have done better!

"And they couldn't have done better than this, either," Booster joked to Bleep later on that night.

"Give us another slice of Star Cake!" And both boys tucked in heartily and settled down with their Space Cub friends to watch the brilliant sky at Bleep's Exploding Stars Night Party!

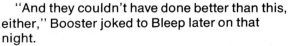

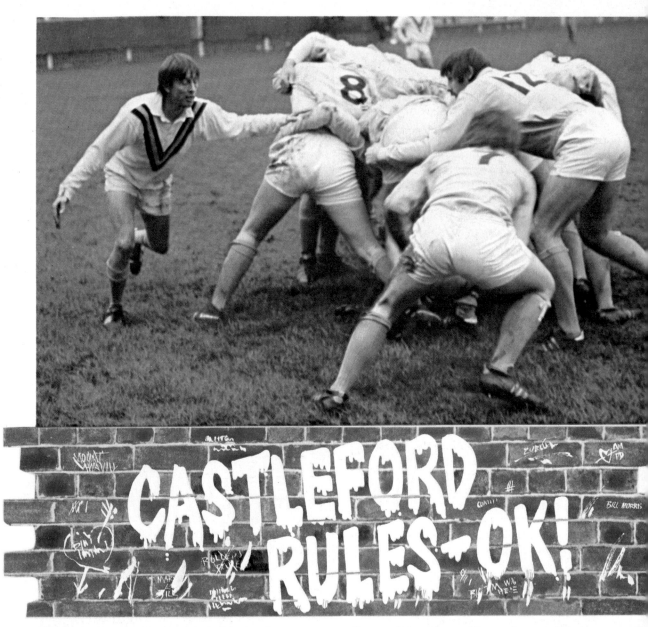

CASTLEFORD RULES - OK!

For most people there are two kinds of football—Rugby and Soccer—but up in the north of England, where I come from, there's a third, and for me it's the toughest of the lot.

Rugby League is as northern as tripe and onions. Until it appeared on BBC *Grandstand*, very few people south of Wakefield had ever heard of it. It's a spin-off from the old Rugby Union—the gentleman's game that's strictly amateur, which means the players don't get paid. In the north, where colliers and iron workers used to work six days a week, they couldn't get time off to play and practise without having their money stopped, so the clubs agreed to pay them for the shift they'd lost and that caused a split with the Rugby Union whose members could afford to play for nothing. That all happened back in the 1890s, but Rugby League has survived and is a semi-pro game to this day.

The Castleford team all have different jobs during the week. The captain, Malcolm Reilly, sells oil; Trevor Briggs, the wing three-quarter, is a policeman; and Bruce Burton, the chief try-scorer, works for a deep-freeze company. Goal-kicker

Sammy Lloyd is a collier, so it was after he came off shift that I joined him for some goal-kicking practice on the vast Castleford ground.

He was taking endless shots at the uprights from every possible angle. Sammy is handsome, six feet tall and weighs 15 stone. When he tackles you it's like being hit by an express train.

"I like to get *involved* in the game, John," he said with a charming smile.

I asked him what it was like taking a penalty three minutes before the end of a match when your kick could win the game.

"Well, it can be pretty tough, especially when you're away from home with two thousand opposing fans breathing down your neck. But you've got a job to do—so you just get on with it."

Captain Malcolm Reilly, who's the chief coach as well, came trotting on the field with the rest of the team.

"Right, lads. Let's have some tacklin' practice!"

A huge tractor tyre—almost as tall as me—was bowled on to the pitch. The tyre was an opposing winger—and we had to bring him down before he

To play Rugby League you've got to be tough—and that means training.

I hoped the opposition was going to be smaller than this tractor inner tube.

The winning smile of Sammy Lloyd, the chief goal kicker, who works down the pit.

There was no turning back now—in five minutes time I would be out on the field.

crossed the line.

"Come on, Johnny, more aggression!" Malcolm yelled as I launched myself at this ludicrous black bowling monster. It really looked very sinister trundling out of the darkness into the floodlit area. All regular training has to be done at night as that's the only time when everyone is free.

The session lasted an hour, and I felt pretty shattered after it. I thought there was nothing that a pie and a plateful of mushy peas in the clubroom couldn't put right, but I felt a bit of a twinge in my thigh when I came out of the bath, and Malcolm noticed I was limping.

"You'd better go and see the physio, lad," he said.

The physio was John Malpas, an old Castleford player, whose duty now was to keep the team fighting fit for the rugby season.

I stripped off and lay on my front while John oiled and pummelled my back into condition. In between groans, I asked him if they ever had any really serious injuries.

"One or two get their collar-bones done in—but they're a pretty tough bunch, you know!"

"Yes, I noticed that," I said.

Malcolm put his head round the door.

"Will he be fit for Saturday?" he asked.

"Saturday?" I said—panic beginning to rise.

"Don't worry, lad, we're not thinking of playing against Wigan—but we don't want to send you back to London before you've experienced a game."

The game was a special friendly match that they'd organised for Saturday morning.

I hardly dared tell them, but I'm a Rugby Union man. I played quite a bit as scrum half when I was at school—but that was a year or two ago, and it's quite a different game. The basic idea's the same. You've got to put the ball down on the opposing team's line, and if you succeed, you can have a go at kicking a goal. But there are all kinds of little differences in the rules, and there are two men less on each side, which makes the whole game faster and involves a lot more running. The average winger runs about five miles flat out in the course of an 80-minute match.

The teams were a mixture of the first and 'A' teams. It was Castleford versus Castleford, but Eddie Waring, who'd come to do the commentary, dubbed my team the "Noakes Nomads"—and the name stuck.

"What position are you playing, John?" he asked me before the game.

"Scrum half," I replied.

"Well, you've got some courage, I'll say that! When Mal Reilly comes round that pack, you'll need to get a bit of a move on."

I walked back towards the dressing-room.

"John," called Eddie, "don't go for the up and unders, lad."

Sammy, who was on my side, fell into step with me.

"'Ave you got a mouth guard?" he asked.

"No," I said. . . .

Sammy gave me his winning smile.

"You'll need one," he said.

The ref. told me the kind of signs he'd be giving during the game. I asked him how many warnings he

After 80 minutes of running and being jumped on, there's nothing in the world like a Rugby bath!

gave before sending a player off.

"Well, if it's a bad foul—like a fellow losing a couple of teeth—you send them off straight away!"

In the dressing-room, I began to feel very puny as I looked at the massive frames of the other players.

"Some of these lads wear shoulder pads under their shirts," said Geoff Wraith, the full back. He looked as big as a house.

"Do you?" I asked.

"No," he grinned. "I reckon I'm big enough."

"Do you wear a mouth guard?" I continued.

"I used to, but I've given that up as well."

"Oh, why?" I asked.

"Well, I lost all my front teeth last season," he gaped.

On that note of reassurance, I laced up my boots and ran out on to the pitch.

". . . And the crowd here at Wheldon Road gives quite a roar as the 'Noakes Nomads' take the field," commented Eddie Waring.

The word had got around the town that Noakes was daft enough to take on Castleford, so a lot of Blue Peter viewers had turned up for the kill.

The scrum half's job is to put the ball in the scrum and then run round the pack hoping that your hooker will have heeled it out. Then you pick it up and pass it to one of the wingers, who could start a move towards the enemy line. Judging when to put the ball into the scrum is very critical, and you must put it in straight, or the ref. will award a penalty to the opposing team. I got ragged by Eddie Waring for flinging myself on the ground when I made my pass.

"John Noakes is giving us a Rugby *Union* pass.

But Dennis Hartley gathers it, and neatly side-steps a burly forward. Hartley passes to Kear, Kear to Garbutt, back to Kear, and back to Noakes. Oh, a lovely feint to his left—and he's over!"

I was buried under about 100 stones of "muscle and bone" as Eddie would say, but I didn't care—I'd scored.

By half-time our team had a lead of ten points to nil. I was over the moon, but John Sheridan, the 'A' team coach, was still worried.

"Right, lads, we're not doing badly in this first half. Ten good points that. But what's happening in the scrum? We're getting plenty of the ball—but we seem to be shoving round all the time."

There was silence on the bench.

"Am I putting it in too late?" I asked.

Dennis Hartley said: "We do seem to be labouring as it's coming in. If you could put it in that bit quicker, then we'd have more chance."

I hardly seemed to have sat down, let alone sucked my lemon, and we were on the field again. I took quite a bit of punishment in that second half. I was getting more and more tired, and when you're tired you're slow—and when you're slow you get hammered.

In the end we lost, 19 points to 13.

"Well played, Castleford," said Eddie as we walked back to the dressing-room. "And what shall we say about the scrum half—John Noakes, the Halifax player. Well, he stayed to the end, he scored a try and he got a goal. But I'll bet he's looking forward to the solace of the bath."

"You're right, Eddie!" I was.

"REMEMBER, LESLEY, IT'S SPEED THAT COUNTS!"

"Can you drive a car?" asked Biddy Baxter.
"Ride a horse?" said Rosemary Gill.
"How about skating?" queried Edward Barnes.

That was when I went for my first interview about being on Blue Peter five years ago. I had to say "no" to all those questions and quite a few more as well. Come to think of it, I was pretty lucky to get that job!

Once I started, they all said I really must learn to drive as soon as possible because there's always something that needs to be driven on Blue Peter. I didn't want to be "the little woman" and leave all the driving to John and Peter, so I started lessons, and I'm proud to say I passed my test first go. After that I became quite interested in driving and I've taken every chance I could to try to become a really *good* driver.

You can imagine how delighted I was when I heard that Blue Peter was going to compete in a "stages" rally on Exmoor. And not only that, but I was going to join Jackie Smith to make up the only all-woman crew in the competition.

Jackie is only 22, but she already had two years' rally driving experience. During the week she's a teacher at a primary school in Letchworth, but every weekend she's wearing a crash helmet, strapped in behind the wheel of her Fiat 127. I was going to be Jackie's navigator for the rally, but I joined her the day before so that I could pick up some tips before the rally started.

We were doing a cool 60 mph along the kind of cart track that I would have been reluctant to drive my own car along at 5 miles an hour! The Fiat has a very low road clearance and there was an ominous scraping and bumping noise every time we went over a rock.

"That's the bottom of the car actually touching the ground, Lesley," said Jackie as she gripped the wheel and brought us round the hairpin in a flurry of flying stones.

"That's why we have a sump guard on. Driving an ordinary car on roads like this, you'd probably have a hole in your sump by now and you'd have lost all your oil."

Jackie told me that the whole object of a rally is speed. Every rally is made up of different stages. There were going to be 15 in ours. The cars enter the stages at minute intervals, and the idea is to go as fast as you can to the end.

Some stages are through forests, some along mountain sides, others along country lanes. The

The scrutineer checks every inch of the car to make sure it's safe before you are allowed to start.

The navigator must "read the road" to the driver so I had a last-minute look at the map.

object is to test the drivers on as many different kinds of terrain as possible.

As we sped through the forest, I asked Jackie what exactly I would be doing on the day of the rally.

"You've got to keep one eye on the map and one eye on the road—and really read the road. If there's a bend coming up, you tell me—and by looking at the map, you shout out if it's a left- or a right-hander."

"Right, Jackie, there's a hill coming up with a right-hand bend at the bottom."

Jackie smartly changed down to third, shot down the hill and approached the bend at a speed which looked certain to take us straight through the hedge. At the last second she jammed on the hand brake and put the wheel on full lock, and we broadsided round the corner without losing any speed at all.

"Wow!" I said. It seemed the only possible comment.

When we came to a straight bit, Jackie slowed down and said: "If you're going to be a navigator, you've got to find out what it's like being the driver, so move over."

In the short time I'd been with her I'd built up a complete confidence in Jackie as a driver. John Noakes always says: "Put yourself in the hands of the experts and you won't come to much harm!" But now it was going to be *me* behind the wheel with the expert in the passenger seat!

I gripped the wheel and drove as fast as I could. The car, which had been specially prepared for rally driving, had a fine positive response, and after a while I felt I wasn't doing too badly until Jackie said: "That's fine, Lesley. But you've got to remember that it's speed that counts. From the moment the Start Marshal gives you the go, you're racing against time."

At 6.30 a.m. on the day of the rally Jackie and I arrived at the start. The rally wasn't due to begin until half-past eight, but there was a lot to be done before then. Every car has to be thoroughly checked by a scrutineer. This is mainly for safety to make sure that everything is firmly bolted down and the wall which separates the engine from the passengers is thoroughly fire-proofed. But the scrutineer also makes sure that the engine is the size you've said it

Our helmets were checked to make sure they were strong enough.

is, and there are no illegal gadgets that might give you an unfair advantage. He even checked our helmets to make sure they had the British standard number which guaranteed that they'd been tested to withstand the kind of impact we could suffer in the event of a crash.

Once we'd been scrutinised we drove to a specially guarded car park. No one is allowed to touch the cars between scrutineering and the start, just in case somebody does a spot of engine-switching before the rally!

There were 47 cars in the rally and we were number 47—the last away. It's the moments *before* something begins that are always the worst—like walking into the hall before you start an exam, or waiting in the playground on the first day of school, or when the Floor Manager shouts "30 seconds studio" before every Blue Peter goes on the air. It was just like that at the start of the rally. Jackie, who is extremely pretty with a really lovely smile, was suddenly very quiet and drawn, looking straight ahead. She'd turned a car over in a rally last year, and in those long seconds before the start I guessed she was reliving the moment before the crash and praying that it wasn't going to happen again.

We were number 47, the last car to be clocked out by the Start Marshal.

Jackie suddenly went quiet as tension mounted before the start.

Seconds saved on a bend could make all the difference.

The Start Marshal put the clock on our bonnet, wrote down the time, handed me a copy, and we were off!

All rally cars are restricted to 30 miles per hour on the public roads between the stages, so this breakneck race begins with a leisurely crawl, with the real Sunday motorists flying past the seasoned rally drivers! But once you reach the open country the sky's the limit—provided you can keep the car on the road! We were making pretty good time on the first stage, and Jackie was driving magnificently. I was doing my very best to "read the road".

"Tree stump on your side."

"Thank you."

"100 yards of straight, Jackie—then a hairpin—to the left. Steep right-hand turn at the top of the hill."

"Right."

"—and a nasty drop on my side!"

"Got it!"

Every car is clocked in and out of the various stages and logged by the Marshal, who gives the navigator a copy so that he (or she in my case) can keep a running tot and tell the driver how they're going.

But, of course, you've no idea how the others are getting on. You don't find that out until the end.

We reached the start of the final stage in the pouring rain. Our lime-green car had turned into a uniform mid-brown, and the windscreen was two semi-circles carved out of the mud.

"Are we the last through?" Jackie asked the dripping Marshal.

"No," he said. "Your time's going to be 16.28. Stand by—Five, four, three, two, one—go!"

The end was almost anti-climax. There was no chequered flag or magnum of champagne for the winner. You clock out of the final stage and wait for the Marshals to do their sums. I had to go before the result was declared, but the following day this letter arrived at the Blue Peter office.

Dear Lesley,

I thought I would write to let you know how much I enjoyed our days driving together, I hope I wasn't too bossy. You will be pleased to know that we achieved second place in our class and may possibly receive a small trophy. Surely this must prove your ability as a navigator, what are you doing next weekend?

Joking apart I enjoyed the weekend tremendously and would like to thank you and the Production team for everything that you did to help me.

I hope we have the opportunity of meeting again sometime in the future.

Best wishes,
Jackie Smith.

SOLUTIONS

PUZZLE PICTURES

1 This lavatory is a vital piece of submarine equipment. The lever on the right has five positions: discharge, pause, shut, pause, flushing. The penalty paid by those not positioning the lever in the right order is called by the Navy "getting one's own back".

2 James Galway, the man with the golden flute, played two tin whistles simultaneously when he visited the Blue Peter studio.

3 Turkish Earthquake S.O.S.! Blue Peter viewers donated a plane load of blankets for the disaster victims.

4 The replica of **Stephenson's Locomotion** built for the 150th anniversary celebrations of the Stockton Darlington railway.

5 Taking tea **inside the piston of the world's largest working beam engine** at Kew.

6 Colour Separation Overlay produced these eight John Noakes's, and an electronic voice synthesiser produced nine matching voices.

7 Treble trouble for John and Peter when they helped "Likely Lad" Rodney Bewes bath his 5½-month-old triplets. **John baths Billy, Rodney baths Tom and Peter baths Jack.**

8 A rehearsal for the Stretcher Obstacle Race from the **999 Jamboree.**

9 Fifteen-year-old **Paul Newman, Britain's youngest Punch & Judy man,** who once swallowed his swazzle, shows John the secret of his sausages.

10 The world's most elaborate bucket—**Marie Antoinette's milk pail**, made not from wood but the finest Sèvres porcelain, and for the last hundred years hidden away at Mentmore Towers, the ancestral home of the Duke of Rosebery. (The bucket fetched £60,000 at the Mentmore auction.)

TWIN TOWNS (page 41)
Bordeaux (1) is twinned with **Bristol** (7)
Richmond (2) with **Fontainebleau** (5)
Cambridge (3) with **Heidelberg** (4)
Portsmouth (6) with **Haifa** (8)

THE CASE OF THE TANGLED TAPE

1 As Kaustovich was at a meeting and did not see the British pair skating, he would not have known about the bagpipes, unless he had switched the tapes.

2 Kaustovich could only have known what Giorgio had for supper if he had been into the control room during the time Giorgio went to get the tools, so he had the opportunity to switch the tapes.

3 If Kaustovich had really been a judge, he would have known the Winter Olympics have never been held at Aviemore.

4 Aviemore is in the Cairngorms, not the Pennines.

5 Anyone interested in skating would know John Curry is not a *pairs* skater.

6 No one scores more than six maximum points in the Winter Olympics. 9.8 is impossible.

PUZZLES (page 39)

What's in Store?—1) Rice, 2) Plum Jam, 3) Ginger Snaps, 4) Baked Beans, 5) Salad Cream, 6) Fish Fingers.
Which gadget hasn't got a plug?—No. 5.
TV Programmes: 1) Playaway, 2) Jackanory, 3) Grandstand, 4) Top of the Pops, 5) Multicoloured Swap Shop, 6) Nationwide, 7) Match of the Day, 8) Tomorrow's World, 9) Panorama 10) Crackerjack.
Odd Man Out: No. 7.
Message: Jack and Jill's Birthday was on Saturday, 29th January.

USEFUL INFORMATION

The Rugby Football League:
180 Chapeltown Road, Leeds LS7 4HT.
British Amateur Gymnastic Association:
23a High Street, Slough, Bucks.
Gary Fridd's Sword:
bought by and exhibited at the Yorkshire Museum, Museum Gardens, York. Open: 10.00-16.45 hrs; Sunday 13.00-16.45 hrs.
Lifeline Lebanon:
Any spare stamps and postcards can be sent to: 157 Clapham Road, London SW9 0PT.

ACKNOWLEDGEMENTS

Queen Elizabeth Slept Here, A Tale of Two Cities—Warsaw and Coventry, and *The King's Appendix* were written by Dorothy Smith; Illustrations for *Queen Elizabeth Slept Here* and *Six Brave Men* were by Robert Broomfield; *Bleep & Booster* and the *Mystery Picture* by "Tim"; *Concorde* cutaway by Geoffrey Wheeler.

All photographs in this book were taken by Joan Williams, Barry Boxall, John Jefford, John Adcock, Mike Ward, Charles Walls, Paul Wheeler and Tibor Szalma, with the exception of Dulles Airport (p.23) by Image in Industry; Concorde in flight (p.24) by British Airways; Gourd (p.33) by Syndication International; Cambridge (p.41) by Camera Press; Fontainebleau (p.41) by Picturepoint; Helicopter (p.44) by *The Times*; Gary Fridd (p.59) by Pick of York; Teapot (p.63) by City Museums, Stoke-on-Trent, and remaining pictures on pages 63 & 64 by Radio Times Hulton Picture Library.

BIDDY BAXTER, EDWARD BARNES AND ROSEMARY GILL WOULD LIKE TO ACKNOWLEDGE THE HELP OF GILLIAN FARNSWORTH AND MARGARET PARNELL. DESIGNED BY EILEEN STRANGE AND JOHN STRANGE.

BLUE PETER COMPETITION

Would you like to come to the Television Centre and see the Blue Peter studio? Would you like to meet John, Peter and Lesley—and all the pets?

This could be *your* chance to come to London and meet them all at a special party!

Just solve this puzzle. Here's what you have to do:

Turn to page 22 and study carefully the pomanders Lesley's made. Here's the question: How many cloves has she used to make *all* the pomanders shown on the page? Ignore the drawing—that doesn't count—but don't forget the cloves in the little photo!

Twenty-four people who give the correct answer will be invited to our

and there'll be lots of competition badges for the runners-up, too!

When you've finished clove guessing, write your answer on the entry form and send it to:
Blue Peter Competition,
BBC Television Centre,
London W.12.

First prize winners and runners-up will be notified by letter. The closing date for entries is 15 January 1978.

Lesley used . . . . cloves to make the pomanders.

Name ......N'icola cox...... **Age**...5...

Address 3.wendover Road

Wolverhampton 0907 7alt A16

Published by the British Broadcasting Corporation
35 Marylebone High Street, London W1M 4AA
ISBN 0 563 17287 8 First Published 1977
© British Broadcasting Corporation and John Grant 1977
Printed in England by Purnell & Sons Ltd, Paulton (Bristol)
and London